Comptroller's Handbook

Safety and Soundness

| Capital Adequacy (C) | Asset Quality (A) | Management (M) | Earnings (E) | Liquidity (L) | Sensitivity to Market Risk (S) | Other Activities (O) |

Liquidity

June 2012

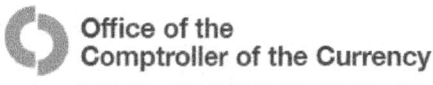

Office of the Comptroller of the Currency

Washington, DC 20219

Liquidity

Contents

This booklet provides guidance to examiners and bankers on assessing the quantity of liquidity risk exposure and the quality of liquidity risk management. The sophistication of a bank's liquidity management process depends on its business activities and appetite for risk, as well as the overall level of liquidity risk. A well-managed bank, regardless of size and complexity, must be able to identify, measure, monitor, and control its exposure to liquidity risk in a timely and comprehensive manner. Liquidity core procedures can be found in the Community Bank Supervision Handbook (January 2010) and in Examiner View (EV). This handbook provides examiners with supplemental procedures for further analyzing the quantity and quality of liquidity risk. Examiners should refer to the Bank Supervision Process Handbook for further guidance on CAMELS Rating System. Additional guidance, particularly for those examiners responsible for examining large and internationally active banks, is provided in the September 2008 "Principles for Sound Liquidity Risk Management and Supervision," issued by the Basel Committee on Banking Supervision (BCBS)[1] and formally adopted by the OCC and other U.S. banking regulatory agencies in that same year.

Background

Traditionally, banks have relied on local retail deposits (transaction and savings accounts) to support asset growth. Most retail deposit balances are federally insured, stable, and relatively inexpensive. Funding dynamics at community, midsize, and large banks, however, have evolved over time. Technological advances in the delivery of financial products and services, the removal of interstate banking restrictions, and the deregulation of interest rates paid on deposit accounts changed both depositor and banker behavior. Legislative reforms were intended to give depository institutions the tools to compete with other market participants for deposits, but they also increased competition among the banks themselves. The combination of these reforms and technological advances also made it easier for depositors, looking for

---

[1] The Basel Committee on Banking Supervision consists of senior representatives of bank supervisory authorities and central banks in Argentina, Australia, Belgium, Brazil, Canada, China, France, Germany, Hong Kong Special Administrative Region, India, Indonesia, Italy, Japan, Luxembourg, Mexico, the Netherlands, Russia, Saudi Arabia, Singapore, South Africa, South Korea, Spain, Sweden, Switzerland, Turkey, the United Kingdom, and the United States. It usually meets at the Bank for International Settlements (BIS) in Basel, Switzerland, where its permanent Secretariat is located.

better returns on their money, to leave their local markets. Consequently, in some cases, retail bank deposit growth did not keep pace with asset growth. Some banks became reliant on alternative deposit, nondeposit, and off-balance-sheet funding sources to cover the shortfall in traditional retail deposit funding.

Changes in technology, product innovation, and funding dynamics create new challenges for liquidity managers. Intense competition and declining customer loyalty increase the rate sensitivity of traditional retail deposits. As banking customers are now using deposit accounts more as transaction vehicles than savings vehicles, thereby maintaining lower average excess balances, bankers can no longer rely upon historically inelastic depositor behavior. Thus, the reliance on alternative sources of funding from the wholesale and brokered markets exposes banks to more rate and liquidity sensitivity than the reliance on traditional retail deposits did. Moreover, many banks have increased their use of products with embedded optionality on both sides of the balance sheet, which makes it more challenging to manage the corresponding cash flows. Liquidity risk management systems and controls must keep pace with these changes and added complexities.

Given these changes in funding dynamics, liquidity management is more complex and requires a more robust risk management process. To effectively identify, measure, monitor, and control liquidity risk exposure, well-managed banks supplement traditional liquidity risk measures like static-balance-sheet ratios with more prospective analyses. Bankers and examiners should have, at a minimum, a sound understanding of a bank's

- projected funding sources and needs under a variety of market conditions.
- net cash flow and liquid asset positions given planned and unplanned balance sheet changes.
- projected borrowing capacity under stable conditions and under adverse scenarios of varying severity and duration.
- highly liquid asset[2] and collateral position, including the eligibility and marketability of such assets under a variety of market environments.
- vulnerability to rollover risk.[3]

---

[2] Defined as the sum U.S. Treasury and Agency securities and excess reserves at the Federal Reserve

[3] Rollover risk is the risk that a bank is unable to renew or replace funds at reasonable costs when they mature or otherwise come due.

- funding requirements for unfunded commitments over various time horizons.
- projected funding costs, as well as earnings and capital positions under varying rate scenarios and market conditions.

Definition

Liquidity is a financial institution's capacity to readily meet its cash and collateral obligations at a reasonable cost. Maintaining an adequate level of liquidity depends on the institution's ability to efficiently meet both expected and unexpected cash flows and collateral needs without adversely affecting either daily operations or the financial condition of the institution. A bank's liquidity exists in its assets readily convertible to cash, net operating cash flows, and its ability to acquire funding through deposits, borrowings, and capital injections.

By definition, *liquidity risk* is the risk that an institution's financial condition or overall safety and soundness is adversely affected by an inability (or perceived inability) to meet its obligations. An institution's obligations, and the funding sources used to meet them, depend significantly on its business mix, its balance sheet structure, and the cash flow profiles of its on- and off-balance sheet obligations. In managing its cash flows, an institution confronts various situations that can give rise to increased liquidity risk. These include funding mismatches, market constraints on the ability to convert assets into cash or in accessing sources of funds (i.e., market liquidity), and contingent liquidity events. Changes in economic conditions or exposure to credit, market, operational, legal, and reputation risks also can affect an institution's liquidity risk profile and should be considered in the assessment of liquidity and asset or liability management.

In assessing a bank's liquidity position, examiners should consider a bank's access to funds as well as its cost of funding. Depending on the current interest rate and competitive environments, undue reliance on wholesale or market-based funding may increase a bank's cost structure. The cost of acquiring or renewing such funding is purely market driven, as opposed to rates paid on retail deposits, which may be set at management's discretion within the parameters of local and national market conditions. Rising or high funding costs, especially in comparison to peer and market rates, is a sign of potential liquidity problems.

Importance of Liquidity Management

Liquidity is the lifeblood of any institution, but it is particularly crucial to highly leveraged entities such as banks. More broadly, the financial crisis beginning in 2008 demonstrated how liquidity problems and risks can be transmitted throughout the entire financial system. For all banks, the immediate and dire repercussions of insufficient liquidity makes liquidity risk management a key element in a bank's overall risk management structure.

The OCC expects all banks to manage liquidity risk with sophistication equal to the risks undertaken and complexity of exposures. Critical elements of a sound liquidity risk management process established by the board include

- appropriate corporate governance and active involvement by management.
- appropriate strategies, policies, procedures, and limits used to manage and control liquidity risk, even in stressed conditions.
- appropriate liquidity risk measurement and monitoring systems.
- active management of intraday liquidity and collateral.
- maintaining an appropriately diverse mix of existing and potential future funding sources.
- adequate levels of highly liquid marketable securities, with no legal, regulatory, or operational impediments, that can be used to meet liquidity needs in stressful situations.
- comprehensive contingency funding plans (CFP) sufficient to address potential adverse liquidity events and emergency cash flow needs.
- adequate internal controls surrounding all aspects of liquidity risk management.

Sources of Liquidity

Structural changes in banks' deposit bases have prompted banks to take advantage of improved access to wholesale and market-based funding sources. Examples of alternative funding sources include federal funds lines, repurchase agreements (repos), correspondent bank lines, Federal Home Loan Bank (FHLB) advances, Internet deposits, deposit-sharing arrangements, and brokered deposits. Access to these funds providers enables banks to meet funding requirements while still maintaining adequate funding diversification. Funds from the wholesale markets can be accessed at a variety of tenors that provide bankers with greater flexibility to manage their cash flows and liquidity needs.

On the other hand, too much reliance on wholesale and market-based funding sources elevates a bank's liquidity risk profile. Bankers who are unfamiliar with wholesale funding markets may become overly complacent during stable economic times. Funding through alternative sources exposes banks to the heightened interest-rate and credit sensitivity of these funds providers. Providers of wholesale funding often require a bank's more liquid assets as collateral, which may impair the overall liquidity of a bank's asset base. Further, if that collateral becomes less liquid, or its value becomes uncertain, wholesale funds providers may be unwilling to extend or roll over funding at maturity. A bank's financial condition as well as market or systemic events unrelated to the institution may adversely affect the cost to a bank to acquire funds or its ability to access the wholesale markets. As a bank's reliance on wholesale and market-based funding increases, so should the quality of liquidity risk-management processes. These processes should include periodic assessments of a bank's exposure to changes in market conditions, and a bank should develop corresponding risk control systems to accompany these assessments.

Asset sales and securitization are also important sources of bank liquidity. Banks of all sizes have increased the use of asset sales and securitization to access alternative funding sources, manage concentrations, improve financial performance ratios, and more efficiently meet customer needs. Some of these transactions, however, carry explicit recourse[4] provisions within contractual documents, as well as the potential implied recourse associated with a bank's desire to maintain access to future funding by repurchasing or otherwise supporting securitizations that exhibit performance problems. As a result, examiners should be aware of situations in which banks might overestimate the risk transfer of sales and securitization or may underestimate the commitment and resources required to manage this process effectively. Such mistakes may lead to highly visible problems during the life of a transaction that could impair future access to the secondary markets. A bank's role and level of involvement in asset sales and securitization activities determine the degree of risk to which it is exposed.

Off-balance-sheet positions can serve as both a source of liquidity and a potential, sometimes unexpected, drain on liquidity. Banks with a substantial amount of unfunded loan commitments may be required to fund such obligations unexpectedly and on short notice. Other off-balance-sheet commitments, such as legally binding and nonlegally binding support for

---

[4] Recourse represents the right of the investor to seek payment from the originator.

securitizations, asset-backed commercial paper conduits, and other market-based funding vehicles, can affect a bank's liquidity position. In addition, collateral required for covering adverse mark-to-market changes in derivative hedging and trading activities may reduce the stock of liquid assets. Often, the fulfillment of nonlegally binding off-balance-sheet commitments is necessary to preserve the reputation of the institution, as well as to allow a bank continued access to that segment of the financial markets. On the other hand, off-balance-sheet activities may provide additional sources for liquidity. Banks can supplement their liquidity position by maintaining lines of credit with correspondent banks or their respective FHLB. Sound liquidity management includes the analysis of and planning for the operational and contingent sources and uses of funds associated with off-balance-sheet activities.

Relationship of Liquidity Risk to Other Banking Risks

Bankers and examiners must understand and assess how a bank's exposure to other risks may affect its liquidity. The OCC defines and assesses eight categories of risk. In addition to liquidity, these risk types include credit, interest rate, price, operational, compliance, strategic, and reputation. These categories are not mutually exclusive—any product or service may expose a bank to multiple risks—and a real or perceived problem in any area can erode a bank's liquidity position or affect its funding costs, thereby increasing its liquidity risk. If a bank does not properly manage these exposures, the risks eventually undermine the institution's liquidity position. Both the "Community Bank Supervision" and the "Large Bank Supervision" booklets of the Comptroller's Handbook discuss in detail the OCC's risk definitions and risk assessment process.

Managing liquidity involves estimating present and future cash needs and providing for those needs in the most cost-effective way possible. Banks obtain liquidity from both sides of the balance sheet, as well as from off-balance-sheet activities. A manager who attempts to control liquidity solely by adjustments on the asset side is potentially ignoring less costly sources of liquidity. Conversely, focusing solely on the liability side or depending too heavily on purchased wholesale funds can leave a bank vulnerable to market conditions and influences beyond its control. Effective liquidity managers consider the array of available sources when establishing and implementing their liquidity plans.

Bank management must understand the sensitivities of their funds providers, the funding instruments they use, the relationship of funding costs to asset yields, and any market or regulatory constraints on funding. In order to accomplish this, management must understand the volume, mix, pricing, cash flows, and risk exposures stemming from its bank's assets and liabilities, as well as other available sources of funds and potential uses of excess cash flow. Management must also be alert to the risks arising from concentrations in funding sources.

Liquidity managers must also understand that a bank's liquidity and liquidity risk profile can change quickly, and these changes may occur outside of management's control. In fact, the adequacy of a bank's liquidity position can be affected by a bank's operating environment or by the market's perception of that institution. A bank's liquidity position may be adequate under certain operating environments yet be insufficient under adverse environments. This is particularly true for a bank that is heavily reliant on wholesale or market-based funding sources. During some adverse operating environments, a bank may see a considerable decline in the availability of funding, an increased need for funds, or a dramatic change in the timing of fund inflows or outflows. Therefore, it is critical for managers to determine the adequacy of liquidity under numerous adverse environments.

Key factors that increase an institution's liquidity risk include poor asset quality, high cash-flow volatility, low levels of liquid assets, high or rising funding costs when compared to the assets they fund, concentrations in funding sources, and dependence on credit- and rate-sensitive providers. Effective liquidity management entails the following elements:

- **Management of operating liquidity**: On an ongoing basis, assessing a bank's current and expected future needs for funds, and ensuring that sufficient funds or access to funds exists to meet those needs at the appropriate time.
- **Management of contingent liquidity**: Providing for an adequate cushion to meet unanticipated cash flow needs that may range from high-probability and low-impact events that could occur in daily operations to low-probability and high-impact events that occur less frequently but may significantly affect an institution's safety and soundness.

A financial institution's liquidity needs depend significantly on the balance-sheet structure, product mix, and cash flow profiles of both on- and off-balance-sheet obligations. External events and internal financial and operating risks (interest rate, credit, operational, legal, and reputation risks) can influence the liquidity profile of an institution.

Bank-specific factors include

- deterioration in asset quality,
- events that affect public reputation or market perception (e.g., accounting scandals, adverse consumer or market events),
- deteriorating earnings performance,
- downgrade in a credit rating,
- aggressive balance-sheet growth, and
- breakdowns in internal systems or controls (fraud).

External factors or events include

- geographical—deteriorating local economic conditions,
- systemic—major changes in national or global economic conditions or dislocations in financial markets,
- financial sector - financial scandal or failure of major firms affecting public confidence,
- market-oriented—price volatility of certain types of assets in response to market events, and
- operational—disturbances to payment and settlement systems or local natural disasters.

Contribution of Balance Sheet Structure to Liquidity Risk

Banks should evaluate the cash flow characteristics, structure, and stability of each major asset and liability category to determine the effect on operating and contingent liquidity risk. This assessment, combined with an evaluation of the interrelationship of these asset and liability accounts, provides the basis for determining the quantity of liquidity risk in the institution.

The cash flow volatility of assets and how quickly they can be converted to cash without incurring unacceptable loss form the basis for evaluating the liquidity contained in a bank's asset base. Several factors influence this evaluation, including the credit, interest rate, and price risk profiles of the asset, as well as the accounting treatment. Exhibit 1 (following page) illustrates the primary assets found on a bank's balance sheet and their relative contribution to meeting a bank's liquidity needs.

Exhibit 1.
Asset Contribution to Meeting Liquidity Needs
(Sell or Pledge)

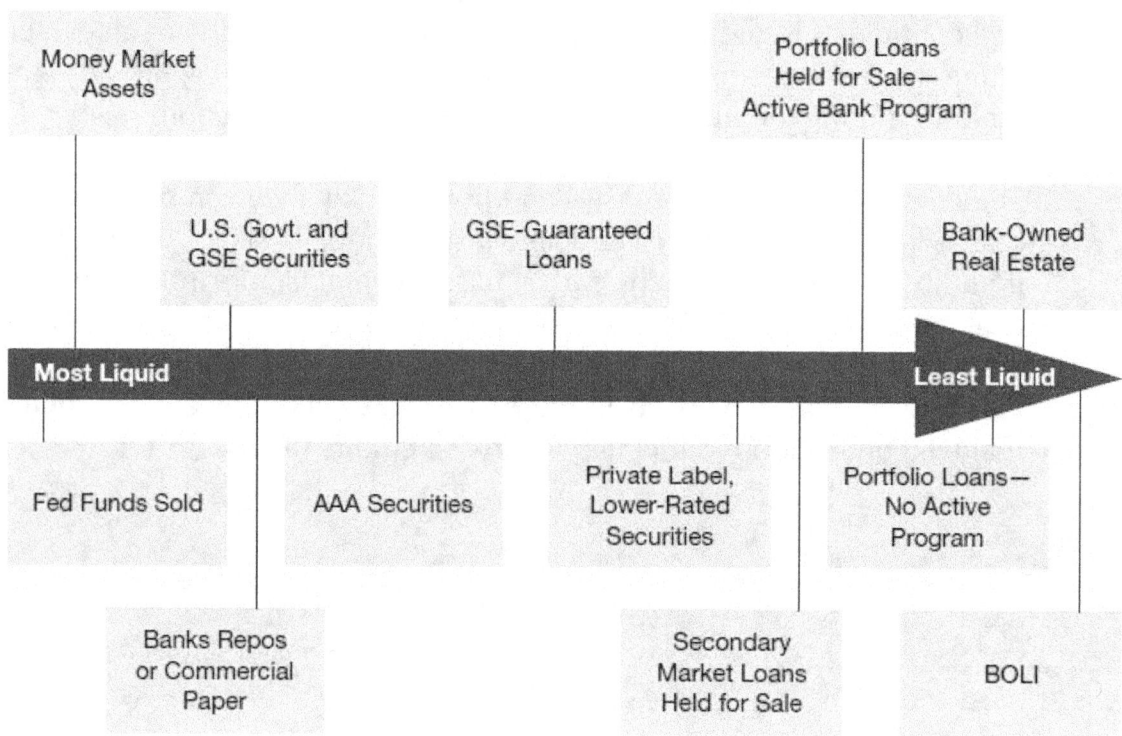

Funding stability of liabilities and the ability to renew or replace them at favorable terms form the basis for assessing the liquidity risk in a bank's liabilities. The stability of a bank's liabilities depends on many factors, including the level of deposit insurance, the degree of credit-risk sensitivity to the institution, and the level of market interest-rate sensitivity. Exhibit 2 (following page) illustrates the primary liabilities on a bank's balance sheet and the relative sensitivity of those funding sources to both interest-rate and credit risk.

Exhibit 2.
Liability Sensitivity

Increasing Credit Sensitivity

Insured Retail Deposits	Uninsured Retail Deposits
Retail Demand Deposits Retail Savings	Retail Demand Deposits Retail Savings
Insured Retail Deposits & Borrowings Money Market Demand Accounts NOW Accounts Certificates of Deposit Collateralized Borrowings Commercial Demand Deposits Secured Public Funds Internet Deposits	**Uninsured Interest-Bearing Deposits & Unsecured Borrowings** Unsecured Borrowings Commercial Paper Eurodollar Deposits Brokered Deposits

Increasing Rate Sensitivity

Banks with large mismatches between liability maturities and asset maturities have greater earnings exposure to changes in interest rates. Changes in market conditions are often unpredictable and sometimes severe. These changes can make it difficult for a bank to secure funds, retain additional funding, and manage the maturity of its funding structure.

Banks that manage liquidity predominantly with liabilities, particularly volatile funding sources, require managers to plan strategies more fully and execute them more carefully than if a bank managed liquidity by relying principally on assets. In these institutions, the interrelationship between liabilities and the assets they fund is critical for sound liquidity risk management. For example, institutions that depend heavily on volatile liabilities with high rollover risk require a higher level of support from liquid assets. Banks that rely on volatile liabilities to fund assets that are less liquid exhibit lower credit quality, or produce less predictable cash flows and possess higher liquidity risk profiles. These banks require well-established funding strategies, such as back-up liquidity lines, contingent calls on equity capital, or a countervailing large, high quality securities portfolio. These banks face the risk that asset cash flows decline at the same time as liabilities mature and roll out of a bank. In addition, if assets with higher credit risk lead to credit quality deterioration and impair a bank's financial condition, some credit-sensitive funding providers may reduce or eliminate their funding to a bank.

Operating Liquidity

A key building block in managing liquidity risk is the estimation of cash inflows (sources of funds) and outflows (uses of funds) for each significant balance-sheet account, given a specific time period. For any given time period, assets and liabilities can have either a net positive or negative impact on cash flows. Specific period aggregate funding mismatches can result in the institution lacking sufficient capacity to fund obligations in the normal course of business (funding gap). Effective management and control of the liquidity risk stemming from funding gaps depends heavily on the use of operational cash flow projections and the reasonableness and accuracy of the assumptions that are applied. Institution-specific factors that affect the development of cash flow assumptions include the following:

- Deteriorating asset quality
- Highly volatile or unpredictable asset amortization (prepayments), non-maturity deposits, off-balance-sheet commitments (lines or letters of credit), and other estimated cash flows
- Unexpected fluctuations in loan demand or deposit balances
- Unanticipated new business due to poor internal management information systems (MIS) reporting and communication
- The inability of permanent takeout lenders to perform as expected.

In order to assess fully the impact of these factors on funding gaps and cash flow projections, management should develop multiple scenarios. These scenarios should include institution-specific risk (i.e., the risk of a credit rating downgrade), market risks such as a market-driven liquidity crisis, and a combination of the two.

Funding mismatches can expose an institution to significant liquidity risk that can be exacerbated by unexpected fluctuations in cash flows under both normal business conditions and stressful contingent events, including swings in collateral required to support off balance sheet derivative contracts. By estimating and reporting future balance-sheet cash flows, management can identify periodic funding mismatches and cash flow shortfalls and excesses. This allows bank management to take steps to generate funds from a bank's asset base or to obtain or attract additional liabilities before actual cash flow mismatches occur.

Asset-Based Liquidity Sources

Liquidity managers may look toward a bank's assets as a source for primary (operating liquidity) and secondary (contingent liquidity) funding. Asset-based liquidity sources include cash flows stemming from a bank's various asset classes, the use of assets as collateral for a variety of funding alternatives, or the securitization or liquidation of assets for cash.

Cash Flows

The primary source of funding stemming from a bank's asset base is the periodic principal and interest cash flows produced by the loan and investment securities portfolios. The cash flow schedules of a bank's assets can be based on their contractual maturity and are predictable and expected, or they may be adjusted by contractual options afforded to the counterparty and occur unexpectedly. A significant impact on a bank's liquidity position typically occurs when counterparties do not pay according to their contractual requirements because of credit problems or other issues.

Pledging of Assets

Financial institutions routinely pledge various types of assets to secure borrowings or line commitments. Secured or collateralized borrowings generally are more reliable sources of liquidity and are generally lower cost when compared with unsecured funding sources. Secured stand-by commitments are also a common form of liquidity provided by the pledging of assets. Common providers of secured funding are the Federal Home Loan Banks, the Federal Reserve discount window, and broker-dealers (repurchase agreements).

While pledging provides a lower cost and a more stable alternative to unsecured borrowings, banks must carefully manage the amount of assets available for pledging. A bank should have the ability to calculate all of its collateral positions, including assets currently pledged relative to the amount of security required and unencumbered assets available to be pledged. A bank's level of available collateral should be monitored by legal entity, by jurisdiction, and by currency exposure. Furthermore, systems should be capable of monitoring shifts between intraday and overnight, or term collateral usage.

Although secured funding providers are less sensitive to a bank's condition and performance than unsecured creditors, credit risk exposure has a significant impact on the ultimate liquidity provided by pledged bank assets. In addition, changes in the following factors may affect counterparty collateral requirements and may force a bank to increase the amount of assets required to secure funding:

- The credit quality, underwriting, or performance of pledged loans
- The liquidity or market value of pledged assets
- The bank's financial condition
- Collateral margin requirements
- The counterparty advance rates on various types of collateral
- The amount of borrowings or collateral pledged when compared with the overall size of the bank (e.g., total assets, total loans)
- Regulatory actions against the bank.

Liquidation of Assets

Banks obtain funds by reducing or liquidating assets. Most institutions incorporate asset liquidation into their ongoing management of operating liquidity. They also use the potential liquidation of a portion of their assets (generally, a portion of their loan or investment portfolio) as a contingent liquidity source under adverse liquidity circumstances. Assets must be unencumbered, be marketable, and have a low interest-rate and price-risk profile to be effective as a contingent liquidity source. The sale of less liquid assets usually requires a bank to engage in an active and ongoing sales program to achieve efficient transactions and favorable market pricing, which limits availability during times of stress.

Securitization of Assets

Asset securitization is another method that some banks use to fund their activities. Securitization involves the transformation of on-balance-sheet loans (e.g., auto, credit card, commercial, student, home equity, and mortgage) into packaged groups of loans in various forms that are subsequently sold to investors. Depending on the business model employed, securitization proceeds can be a material source of ongoing funding and a significant tool for meeting future funding needs. However, for banks that have not previously used securitization as a funding tool, the administrative requirements for securitization may mean significant delays in obtaining funds. In addition, a bank without experience in using securitization may find that its underwriting and administrative policies and procedures do not meet market requirements or expectations. In addition, banks must ensure that their securitization structures and activities comply with all applicable accounting and regulatory guidelines, including those that may be affected by the Dodd–Frank Wall Street Reform and Consumer Protection Act. These activities are sometimes complex and require strong risk management processes. If an institution relies significantly on securitization as a liquidity source, refer to the "Asset Securitization" booklet of the *Comptroller's Handbook* for more information on how to examine these activities. The examination of securitization activities should be closely coordinated with the assessment of liquidity risk.

Liability-Based Liquidity Sources

Liability funding sources are typically characterized as retail or wholesale. Banks distinguish between retail and wholesale funding, because the two sources of funding have different sensitivities to credit risk and interest rates and react differently to changes in economic conditions and the financial condition of a bank.

Retail Deposits

Retail deposits from consumers and small businesses are often important and relatively stable sources of funds for banks. In many instances, the decision made by consumers and business owners to deposit funds in a bank is driven by service and relationship factors, and not merely by the rate of return. Banks focusing on retail deposit generation can build a more diversified and stable funding base, one that is less sensitive to changes in market interest rates and a bank's financial condition. The protection afforded by Federal Deposit Insurance Corporation (FDIC) deposit insurance also provides insured banks with an advantage over other money market participants. During times of bank stress, insured depositors have proven to be a bank's most reliable funding source and, therefore, play an integral role in mitigating liquidity risk during crisis scenarios. Banks can generate interest-bearing retail deposits more quickly by offering interest rates significantly higher than local and national market levels. However, they risk substantially increasing their funding costs if existing customers switch their relationships to the new, higher-cost deposit products. In addition, any new funds generated by high interest rate deposits may prove highly rate sensitive, requiring a bank to match market rates to retain the funding. Noninterest costs can also be substantial. Costs from generating a large volume of new accounts can include personnel, advertising, and operating costs, as well as the costs associated with branch expansion.

Public or municipal deposits are another source for bank funding. Although similar to retail deposits, public deposits are usually in larger denominations, often placed by a professional money manager or through a bidding process and may require collateral in the form of high-quality investment securities. A bank may have existing financial relationships with local municipalities that give the bank a competitive advantage in attracting deposit accounts. Nonetheless, public funds are generally more sensitive to interest rates than retail deposits and often require competitive rates at placement and subsequent rollover dates. Municipalities have a fiduciary responsibility for the safe placement of funds and typically are mandated to place funds only in banks that are sufficiently capitalized and in otherwise sound financial condition. Therefore, public funds are also more sensitive to the financial condition of the depository and may react to a bank's negative press or deteriorating financial condition more rapidly than retail depositors. Liquidity managers must consider these sensitivities of public-funds providers in their operational and contingency planning activities. These products have become more complex over time.

Borrowed Funds

A bank can also generate funds through borrowings from various counterparties. Borrowed funds include secured and unsecured debt obligations across the maturity spectrum. In the short term, borrowed funds include purchased Federal Funds (Fed funds) and securities sold under agreements to repurchase (repos). Longer-term borrowed funds include various types of collateralized loans and the issuance of corporate debt. Depending on their contractual characteristics and the behavior of fund providers, borrowed funds vary in maturity and availability because of their sensitivity to the perceived risk of the institution, general trends in interest rates, and other market factors.

A bank that relies on borrowed funds for ongoing or contingent funding must understand the credit standards of the entities lending to it. Some funds providers may be less sensitive to the financial condition of a bank, since the lenders are primarily focused on the quality and liquidity of collateral, and are looking to the pledged assets to ensure repayment. However, other funds providers, including sellers of overnight funds and the Federal Home Loan Banks, usually have credit policies that lead them to require alternative or additional collateral if the actual or perceived condition of the institution begins to deteriorate. They might also freeze or reduce funding provided to a bank that is experiencing a deteriorating financial condition. Bank management should determine the credit policies of key funds providers and use that information to estimate the amount of funding that would be available to a bank as its financial condition changes. This is an integral part of planning for funding contingencies.

Deposit Listing Services

A bank may use a national deposit listing service to raise both time and money market deposits. This source of funding can be convenient and usually involves minimal noninterest costs. A bank can also tailor the tenor of listed deposits to meet its funding needs. However, it is sometimes difficult to control the volume of funds generated from listing services. Further, funds generated from these sources tend to be more rate sensitive than deposits raised locally, because the relationship with the depositor is based principally on the offering rate. Funding strategies that incorporate deposit listing services should include management systems designed to control these risks. Because the depositor relationship with a bank is motivated primarily through rates paid, deposits obtained through the use of a listing service have behavioral characteristics similar to deposits gathered through a broker. However, they generally do not meet the formal definition of a brokered deposit, because the service merely involves the listing of offering rates and does not employ the use of a third party to communicate with the customer.

Brokered Deposits

Brokered deposits[5] are deposits that are obtained or placed through the use of or relationship with a third party (deposit broker). Banks obtain brokered deposits typically through arrangements with securities brokerage firms. However, brokered deposits can be gathered through other means as well, including a deposit listing service. Brokered deposits can also be obtained through a sweep arrangement with an affiliated broker dealer. While sweep accounts pay a market rate, these accounts are established to maximize

---

[5] See Appendix A, "Brokered Deposit Use and Restrictions," for additional guidance.

insurance coverage. The use of brokered deposits provides a means for banks to raise large amounts of funds quickly with a predetermined maturity structure. However, similar to deposits gathered via a listing service, the primary motivation for placing or depositing funds is the offering rate. These funds are highly rate sensitive. Thus, at maturity, a bank will need to match prevailing market rates to successfully roll over or renew the deposit. Brokered deposits with short-term or immediate (e.g., money market deposit accounts) maturities are particularly at risk to rollover risk and should be closely monitored and managed. For institutions with material reliance on brokered deposits, management must identify and maintain committed alternative funding sources for short-term deposit maturities as conditions warrant. Funding strategies should also address the potential higher costs associated with renewing or replacing funds garnered through a deposit broker. In addition, banks that do not meet regulatory requirements to be "well capitalized" (under Prompt Corrective Action 12 CFR 6) will find their ability to access or renew brokered funds restricted or eliminated, and both primary and contingent funding plans should incorporate this potential loss of funding.

Funding From the Financial Markets

Some banks, particularly larger domestic and multinational institutions, turn to the financial markets for funding. Today, financial markets provide funding to banks in a variety of ways, including asset purchases, repurchase agreements, and equity and debt issuances. These sources provide a broader and more diversified funding base to larger banks. Often these market-based funding programs, when conducted on a broad scale, can allow banks to access funds at costs below those associated with more traditional retail deposit gathering.

A bank's reliance on the financial markets for funding, however, can also increase the level, uncertainty, and complexity of a bank's liquidity risk profile. The acceptance of bank products and services by the financial markets can be affected by a multitude of factors not usually associated with more traditional bank funding strategies. In addition to the customary institution-specific liquidity risks associated with most wholesale funding regimes, funding from financial markets also exposes a bank to heightened systemic liquidity risk. Increased liquidity risks can arise from the volatility of global and domestic funds supply and demand, unexpected disruptions in normal market trading and pricing, settlement and operational interruptions, and pronounced adjustments in a market's risk pricing and acceptance.

Many financial market funding vehicles that remove assets from a bank's balance sheet sometimes carry with them both contractual and noncontractual funding commitments. These noncontractual or implied commitments are usually not exercised during normal market conditions. However, during market disruptions or times of stress, these commitments to financial investors and other market participants may necessitate substantial and unexpected use of funds or require a bank to repurchase underlying assets. Often, the fulfillment of these nonlegally binding commitments is necessary to preserve the reputation of the institution and allow a bank continued access to that segment of the financial markets. When the quality and performance of these assets has deteriorated, this condition may elevate the issuing bank's liquidity risk profile.

When a bank relies on funding from the financial markets, both operating and contingent liquidity management and planning programs must incorporate strategies designed to mitigate these unique and sometimes complex liquidity risks.

Sound liquidity risk management involves the board and senior management's development and oversight of a comprehensive process that identifies, measures, monitors, and controls a bank's liquidity risk exposure. Well-managed banks have their liquidity risk management process integrated into the bank's overall risk management framework.

The key components of a sound liquidity risk management process include

- corporate governance and accountability.
- policies, procedures, and limits.
- risk measurement, monitoring, and reporting systems.
- intraday liquidity management.
- funding diversification.
- maintenance of a cushion of highly liquid assets.
- comprehensive contingency funding plans.
- internal controls.

Corporate Governance

Boards of directors and bank management have the responsibility to implement an effective liquidity risk management process. Both work to ensure that the staffing and structure are commensurate with a bank's level of liquidity risk. A bank should have a reliable management information system designed to provide the board of directors, senior management, and other appropriate personnel with timely and forward-looking information on the liquidity position of the bank.

The board's responsibility centers on setting the strategic direction for the bank. Part of this process includes an assessment of the board's liquidity risk appetite as well as the liquidity required to fulfill strategic initiatives. The board implements policies that govern liquidity risk management under both business-as-usual and stressed conditions. These policies should clearly define the roles and responsibilities of board committees, senior management, and senior management committees with appropriate segregation of duties between execution and oversight of liquidity risk. It is also appropriate for bank policies to define the board's desired risk tolerance by establishing key liquidity risk limits. To ensure that senior management implements the board's stated direction, the board should regularly receive reports that detail a bank's liquidity position and be immediately informed of any material changes in a bank's liquidity risk profile. In multibank holding companies, the board should also understand the liquidity profile of important affiliates and their impact on a bank.

Policies, Procedures, and Limits

Banks should have policies and procedures for identifying, measuring, and controlling liquidity risk exposures. These should translate the board's goals, objectives, and risk tolerances into operating standards. Formal policies and procedures approved by the board should provide a consistent approach to identifying, measuring, and controlling liquidity risk.

Policies should assign responsibility for managing liquidity throughout the bank, including separate legal entities, relevant operating subsidiaries, and affiliates, when appropriate. Policies should also discuss the approach for managing liquidity, set liquidity risk tolerances, and discuss to what extent liquidity risk management will be centralized or decentralized.

Policies communicate how much emphasis a bank places on asset liquidity, liability gathering, and operating cash flows to meet its day-to-day and contingent funding needs. Policies include both quantitative and qualitative targets. Examples include

- definition and minimum level of highly liquid assets.
- elative reliance on both short-term and long-term funding sources, both on an ongoing basis and under contingent liquidity scenarios.
- guidelines or limits on the composition of assets and liabilities.
- level of cash flow mismatches.
- controls over funding costs.
- convertibility of assets into cash to be used as contingent sources of liquidity.

Policies should also identify the primary objectives and methods to use in meeting daily operating cash outflows, providing for seasonal and cyclical cash flow fluctuations, and addressing various adverse liquidity scenarios. This includes formulating plans and courses of actions for dealing with potential temporary, intermediate-term, and long-term liquidity disruptions.

Formal written policies and procedures should define management responsibilities. These should address the lines of authority for the following:

- Developing liquidity risk management policies, procedures, and limits.
- Developing and implementing strategies and tactics used in managing liquidity risk.
- Conducting day-to-day liquidity management.
- Establishing and maintaining liquidity risk measurement and monitoring systems.
- Authorizing exceptions to policies and limits.
- Identifying potential liquidity risk and related issues arising from the introduction of new products and activities.

Policies and procedures should identify the individuals or committees responsible for liquidity risk management decisions. Less-complex banks often assign these responsibilities to the chief financial officer or an equivalent-level senior management official. Other institutions assign responsibility for liquidity risk management to a committee of senior managers, sometimes called a finance committee or asset/liability committee (ALCO). Policies should clearly identify the individual or the committee's duties and responsibilities, the extent of their decision-making authority, and the form and frequency of periodic reports to senior management and the board of directors. When a bank uses an ALCO or other senior management committee, the committee should monitor the liquidity profile of the bank and include representation from all major business lines that can affect liquidity risk (e.g., lending, investment, deposit-gathering, funding, operations). Committee members should include senior managers who have clear authority to execute strategies and transactions that affect liquidity. The committee should ensure that the liquidity risk measurement system identifies and quantifies all primary liquidity risk exposures. They should also ensure that the reporting process communicates accurate, timely, and relevant information about the level and sources of risk exposure.

Liquidity risk tolerances or limits should be consistent with a bank's complexity and liquidity risk profile. Risk tolerances should reflect both quantitative targets and qualitative guidelines. These limits, tolerances, and guidelines may include the following:

- Limits on projected net cash flow positions (sources and uses of funds) over specified time horizons. Projected sources and uses statements are dynamic statements of cash flow and should include on- and off-balance-sheet change projections (e.g., loan growth, deposit outflows). Limits may be placed on liquidity projection ratios (e.g., total projected sources/ total projected uses), or on the capacity coverage ratio (total available secondary funding/net projected cash flow) over various time frames (e.g., daily, weekly, monthly, semiannually, annually).[6]

- Limits on discrete or cumulative funding mismatches or gaps over specified short- and long-term time horizons (e.g., next day, one week, two weeks, one month, six months).[7]
- Target amounts of highly liquid asset reserves expressed as aggregate amounts or as ratios calculated in relation to, for example, coverage of net cash outflows, or expected liquidity needs under stress scenarios.
- Limits or triggers on the structure of short-term and longer-term funding of the asset base, under both normal and stressed conditions.
- Limits or triggers on funding concentrations or guidelines that promote funding diversification such as limits on large liability and borrowed funds dependency, limits on single funds providers, limits on exposure to market segment funds providers, and limits on specific types of brokered deposits or other wholesale funding.
- Limits or triggers on contingent liabilities such as unfunded loan commitments and lines of credit supporting asset sales or securitizations.
- Guidance on the minimum and maximum average maturity of different categories of assets and liabilities.

Banks may use other risk indicators in specifying limits: loans-to-deposit (LTD) ratios; loans-to-equity capital; purchased funds-to-total assets; and other common balance sheet measures and comparisons. In using these measures, however, banks should be fully aware that they might not address the time dimension and scenario-specific characteristics of a bank's liquidity risk profile. Static balance-sheet measures may hide significant liquidity risk that can occur in the future under normal and adverse business conditions. Therefore, they should not be the exclusive measures that banks use to monitor and manage liquidity.

Well-managed banks develop policies governing the creation and maintenance of a written, comprehensive, and up-to-date liquidity contingency funding plan. Policies should also ensure that, as part of ongoing liquidity risk management, senior management identifies early warning indicators of potential liquidity problems.

---

[6] See appendixes B, F, G, and H for examples of these types of reports.

[7] See appendix C, "Liquidity Gap Report," for an example.

Banks should ensure that their policies and procedures take into account compliance with appropriate laws and regulations that can have an impact on an institution's liquidity risk management and liquidity risk profile. These laws and regulations include the Dodd-Frank Act, Federal Deposit Insurance Corporation Improvement Act (FDICIA), the Federal Reserve Act, and certain regulations issued thereunder. Procedures for determining a bank's compliance with certain laws and regulations are included in "Supplemental Procedures: Quality of Risk Management" at the end of this booklet, but this section does not address all laws and regulations that may be applicable.

Liquidity Risk Measurement, Monitoring, and Reporting Systems

A bank's liquidity risk measurement process should be commensurate with its size, complexity, and liquidity risk profile. Similar to a bank's policy limits and targets, the measurement of liquidity should be comprehensive and prospective. To be comprehensive, the measurement of liquidity must incorporate all of the cash flows and liquidity implications from all material assets, liabilities, off-balance-sheet positions and other activities, including the potential optionality embedded in the institution's assets and liabilities. In order for measurement to be prospective, the measurement must be forward-looking by attempting to identify potential future funding mismatches, as well as those that currently exist. Analysis of liquidity should include both quantitative and qualitative factors. This analysis, at a minimum, should address the following:

- The bank's sources and uses of cash and their relevant trends.
- Pro-forma cash flow statements and funding mismatch gaps over different time horizons.
- New products and their affect on liquidity.
- Trends and expectations in the volume and pricing of assets, liabilities, and off-balance-sheet items that may significantly affect the bank's liquidity.
- Trends in the relative cost of funds required by existing and alternative funds providers and the impact on net interest income and margin.
- The diversification of funding sources and trends in funding concentrations.
- Asset quality trends.
- The sensitivity of funds providers to both financial market and institutional trends and events.

- The bank's exposure to both broad-based market and institution-specific contingent liquidity events.
- A discussion of highly liquid assets, trends in those assets, and the market dynamics that could affect their conversion to cash.
- The market's perception of the bank as indicated by excess spread paid relative to similar banks.
- If applicable, the impact of cash flows related to the repricing, exercise, or maturity of financial derivatives contracts, including the potential for counterparties to demand additional collateral in the case of a weakening of the market's perception of the bank.
- If applicable, the impact on cash flows by providing correspondent, custodian, and settlement activities.
- If applicable, the bank's capacity to manage liquidity risk exposures arising from the use of foreign currency deposits and short-term credit lines to fund domestic currency assets, as well as the funding of foreign currency assets with domestic currency.

In addition to a review of the bank's specific sources and uses of funds, measurement of liquidity should also take into consideration relevant national and local trends. These should include the following:

- Economic and financial market developments, such as trends in interest rates and funding costs.
- General credit conditions in the bank's target market.
- General corporate earnings trends and projections.

A fundamental measure of prospective liquidity risk is the projection of the institution's cash flows under alternative scenarios. These projections include business-as-usual scenarios that incorporate relevant seasonality, growth assumptions, or alternative business plans and various adverse stress scenarios. Management's analysis of the trends in the bank's funding sources and balance-sheet structure should be used to develop these cash flow projections. The level of sophistication can range from simple spreadsheets to very detailed analytical reports; these projections should be consistent with the bank's complexity and its liquidity risk profile.

Assumptions play a critical role in the construction of liquidity measures and the development of cash flow projections. Liquidity risk managers need to ensure that all assumptions used are reasonable and appropriate. Key assumptions should be reviewed, documented, and approved annually. Assumptions used in assessing the liquidity risk of assets, liabilities, and off-balance-sheet positions with uncertain cash flows, market values, or maturities should be subject to documentation and review. Banks with material amounts of complex or uncertain cash flows should perform stress tests to determine what effect changes to their material assumptions have on their liquidity profile.

Assumptions surrounding the stability of retail deposits and brokered deposits as well as secondary market borrowings are important, particularly when evaluating the availability of alternative sources under adverse contingent scenarios. Analysis of these assumptions should consider, at a minimum

- historic behavior of deposit customers and other funds providers.
- current and future business conditions that may change the historic responses of customer and funds providers' behavior.
- general conditions and characteristics of the institution's market for various types of funds, including the degree of competition.
- anticipated pricing behavior of funds providers under each scenario.

Banks that rely significantly on secured financing should have strong processes in place to evaluate asset liquidity under a variety of business-as-usual and stress conditions. They should also include a determination of whether the asset is free to be used as collateral, an assessment of market haircuts, market capacity constraints, access to the central bank borrowings, concentrations in collateral, potential name-specific concerns, and the ability to complete the transaction.

Methods used to measure and monitor liquidity risk should be sufficiently robust and flexible to allow for timely computation of the metrics used in ongoing liquidity risk management. Risk monitoring and reporting should be able to provide information for day-to-day risk management and control. Additionally, the frequency and scope of risk monitoring systems should be developed so they are easily expandable during times of stress.

The complexity and sophistication of management reporting and management information systems (MIS) should be consistent with the bank's liquidity risk profile. Liquidity MIS should be sufficiently detailed to allow management to assess the sensitivity of the bank to changes in market conditions, its own financial performance, and other risk factors. Reports may include

- cash flow projections that assess both "business-as-usual" and contingent liquidity scenarios. These may be both static (to identify recent trends) and forward looking (to identify prospective needs).
- funding concentration reports that highlight the dependence on sources of funds that may be highly sensitive to bank-specific contingent liquidity risk.[8]
- critical assumptions employed in cash flow projections and other measures as well as their implications.
- the status of key early warning signals or risk indicators.
- the status of contingent funding sources or collateral usage.
- a selected set of appropriate liquidity ratios that highlight the liquidity risk profile of the bank and trends in these ratios.
- the impact of new product and investment activities.
- measures and ratios tailored to the institution's primary liquidity management and funding strategies, liquidity risk profile, and significant activities.[9]
- When appropriate, both consolidated and unconsolidated liquidity risk reports for banks with multiple offices, international branches, and subsidiaries.

Intraday Liquidity Management

Intraday liquidity monitoring is an important component of the liquidity risk management process for institutions, particularly for those engaged in significant payment, settlement, and clearing activities. An institution's failure to manage intraday liquidity effectively, under normal and stressed conditions, could leave it unable to meet payment and settlement obligations in a timely manner, adversely affecting its own liquidity position and that of its counterparties. Among large, complex organizations, the interdependencies that exist among payment systems and the inability to meet certain critical payments have the potential to lead to systemic

---

[8] Examples of reports on funding concentrations include information on the types and amounts of negotiable certificates of deposit stratified by size and origin (e.g., community or market area; brokered, deposit-splitting networks; Internet-rate listed) and other obligations, as well as the collateral and credit triggers or policies of major wholesale funds providers.

[9] Examples include reports on the quality, pledging status, and maturity distribution of the investment securities portfolio in those banks that are heavily reliant on those assets as a primary source of contingent liquidity. Alternatively, a bank reliant on securitizations or loan sales as a primary source of funding should develop reports that target the liquidity risks inherent in those activities.

disruptions that can prevent the smooth functioning of all payment systems and money markets. Therefore, institutions with material payment, settlement, and clearing activities should actively manage their intraday liquidity positions and risks to meet payment and settlement obligations on a timely basis under both normal and stressed conditions. Senior management should develop and adopt an intraday liquidity strategy that allows the institution to do the following:

- Monitor and measure expected daily gross liquidity inflows and outflows.
- Manage and mobilize collateral when necessary to obtain intraday credit.
- Identify and prioritize time-specific and other critical obligations in order to meet them when expected.
- Settle other less critical obligations as soon as possible.
- Control credit to customers when necessary.

Small institutions must also maintain an appropriate intraday liquidity management process. In these institutions, management must focus on the adequacy of funds and credit within their Federal Reserve (Fed) or correspondent settlement and clearing account. Sound intraday liquidity management ensures the following:

- Active monitoring of significant intraday settlement and clearing activity.
- Maintenance of sufficient cash balances and daylight overdraft capacity, when necessary.
- Adequacy of collateral pledged to the Fed account to cover both expected and unexpected intraday funding needs.
- Incorporation of intraday liquidity maintenance into contingency funding planning and scenarios.

Funding Diversification

An institution should establish a funding strategy that provides effective diversification in the sources and tenor of funding. An institution should diversify available funding sources in the short-, medium- and long-term. Diversification targets should be part of medium- to long-term funding plans and should be aligned with the budgeting and business planning process. Funding plans should take into account correlations between sources of funds and market conditions. Management should also consider the funding implications of any government programs or guarantees that a bank uses. The desired diversification should include limits by counterparty, secured versus unsecured market funding, instrument type, securitization vehicle, and geographic market.

Institutions that rely on market-based funding sources should maintain an ongoing presence in their chosen funding markets and strong relationships with funds providers to promote effective diversification of funding sources. An institution should regularly gauge its capacity to raise funds quickly from each source. The institution should identify the main factors that affect its ability to raise funds and monitor those factors closely to ensure that estimates of fund-raising capacity remain valid.

An essential component of ensuring funding diversity is maintaining market access. Market access is critical for effective liquidity risk management, as this access affects the ability to both raise new funds and liquidate assets. A bank should identify and build strong relationships with current and potential investors, even in funding markets facilitated by brokers or other third parties. Building strong relationships with various key providers of funding can give a bank insight into providers' behavior in times of bank-specific or market-wide shocks. Senior management should ensure that market access is being actively managed, monitored, and tested by the appropriate staff.

An institution should identify diversified alternative sources of funding that strengthen its capacity to withstand a variety of severe institution-specific and market-wide liquidity shocks. Depending on the nature, severity, and duration of the liquidity shock, potential sources of funding include, but are not limited to, the following actions:

Tactical actions
- Sale (either outright or through repurchase agreements) or pledging of liquid assets.
- Drawing-down committed facilities.
- Wholesale deposit growth.
- Lengthening maturities of new liabilities.

Strategic actions
- Retail deposit growth.
- Raising capital.
- Issuance of debt instruments.
- Sale of subsidiaries or lines of business.
- Asset securitization.

Cushion of Highly Liquid Assets

Liquid assets are an important source of both primary (operating liquidity) and secondary (contingent liquidity) funding at many institutions. Indeed, a critical component of an institution's ability to effectively respond to potential liquidity stress is the availability of a cushion of unencumbered highly liquid assets without legal, regulatory, or operational impediments that can be sold or pledged to obtain funds in a range of stress scenarios. These assets should be held to protect against a range of liquidity stress scenarios, including those that involve the loss or impairment of typically available unsecured or secured funding sources. The size of the cushion of such high-quality liquid assets should be supported by estimates of liquidity needs revealed by an institution's stress testing, as well as being aligned with the risk tolerance and risk profile of the institution. Management estimates of liquidity needs during periods of stress should incorporate both contractual and noncontractual cash flows, including the possibility of funds being withdrawn. Such estimates should also assume the inability to obtain unsecured funding and the loss or impairment of access to funds secured by assets other than the safest, most liquid assets.

Management should ensure that highly liquid assets are readily available and are not pledged to payment systems or clearinghouses. The quality of unencumbered liquid assets is important as it ensures accessibility during the time of most need. For example, an institution could use its holdings of high-quality U.S. Treasury securities or similar instruments and enter into repurchase agreements in response to the most severe stress scenarios.

Contingency Funding Plans

A contingency funding plan (CFP) includes policies, procedures, projection reports, and action plans designed to ensure a bank's sources of liquidity are sufficient to fund normal operating requirements under contingent liquidity events. The objectives of the CFP are to do the following:

- Provide a plan for responding to various and increasing levels of a bank's liquidity stress.
- Designate management responsibilities, crisis communication methods and channels, and reporting requirements.
- Identify a menu of contingent liquidity sources that a bank can use under various and increasing adverse liquidity circumstances.

- Describe steps that should be taken to ensure that the bank's sources of liquidity are sufficient to fund scheduled operating requirements and meet the institution's commitments with minimal costs and disruption.

Contingent events arise from both unexpected circumstances and ongoing adverse business conditions. They increase the risk that a bank will not have sufficient funds to meet its liquidity needs. These conditions are caused by bank-specific events or by external occurrences or circumstances. Bank-specific events are usually the result of the unique credit, market, operational, or strategic risks that occur because of a bank's business activities. They can arise from the inability to fund asset growth, the inability to renew or replace maturing liabilities, the exercise of options by customers to withdraw deposits or use off-balance-sheet commitments, and other unforeseen events. External events may be systematic financial market occurrences, such as changes in the price volatility of securities, changes in economic conditions, or dislocations in financial markets.

Contingent liquidity events range from high-probability and low-impact events that occur during the normal course of business to low-probability but high-impact events. These may develop from liquidity pressures that are immediate and short term in nature. They may also present longer-term or sustained situations that may grow over time and have long-term liquidity implications. The duration of an identified stress event is a primary factor when developing contingency plans.

Well-managed banks incorporate planning for high-probability and low-impact liquidity risks into the day-to-day management of their sources and uses of funds. Banks generally accomplish this by assessing possible variations around expected cash flow projections and providing for adequate liquidity reserves and other means of raising funds in the normal course of business.

The CFP primarily addresses low-probability and high-impact events. It addresses both the severity and the duration of negative liquidity events. The CFP should accomplish the following:

- Identify plausible stress events.[10]
- Evaluate those stress events under different levels of severity.

---

[10] See appendix D, "Examples of Liquidity Stress Events, Triggers, and Monitoring Items or Reports," for additional guidance.

- Make a quantitative assessment of funding needs under stress events.[11]
- Identify potential and viable funding sources in response to a stress event.
- Provide for management processes, reporting, and internal as well as external communication throughout the stress event.

Within the CFP, management should identify the stress events that threaten a bank's ability to fund both short-term (e.g., intraday, daily, weekly, monthly) and long-term operating and strategic needs. These events include those situations that have a significant negative impact on the bank's liquidity, earnings, or capital because of its balance-sheet composition, business activities, or management structure. Possible stress events include the following:

- Deterioration in credit quality.
- Decline in the bank's CAMELS composite rating.
- A prompt corrective action capital downgrade.
- Negative press coverage.
- Rising reputation risks.
- Material changes in customer relations and perceptions.
- Actual or threatened adverse action related to the institution's external credit rating.
- Actual or anticipated changes in senior and short-term debt ratings.
- Rapid asset growth, particularly when funded with potentially volatile liabilities.
- Deterioration in financial condition that may jeopardize access to market, wholesale, and central bank funding.
- External events such as natural disasters and disruptions in the markets from which the bank obtains funds.

The CFP scenarios should delineate the various levels of stress severity that could occur during a liquidity crisis. The events, stages, and severity levels should be tailored to the bank's specific funding structure.

A critical element of the CFP is the quantitative projection and evaluation of expected cash flows and the ability of the institution to meet any shortfalls during a stress event. The bank should identify a series of actions it will take during a stress event and commit sources of funds for contingent needs in advance of those stress events. To evaluate a potential stress event, the bank must evaluate the potential erosion in funding as well as the cash flow

[11] See appendix E, "Liquidity Contingency Funding Scenarios," for an example.

mismatches at alternative stages of the stress event. As an event worsens, banks must assume that funding sources could further erode or become cost prohibitive. This evaluation should be based on realistic estimates of funds providers' behavior and collateral expectations and should include both on-balance- and material off-balance-sheet cash flows.

Because a high potential exists for liquidity pressures to spread from one source to another during a significant event, banks should identify alternative sources of liquidity and ensure access to emergency standby funding sources. Banks should conduct advanced planning to ensure that these sources would be readily available. If a bank intends to use asset securitization to meet standby liquidity needs, this planning and analysis should include an assessment of the market's depth and the implications for those markets if the liquidity crisis is the result of a broader market stress event rather than a name-specific event.

The CFP should identify a reliable crisis-management team and administrative structure, including realistic action plans for given levels of stress. It should also be integrated with other contingent planning activities such as the continuity of business planning. It should provide for frequent communication among the crisis team, the board of directors, management, and other interested parties. This communication optimizes the effectiveness of the contingency plan by ensuring that business decisions are coordinated to reduce the impact on a bank's liquidity position. Effective crisis management may also require increased preparation of regular liquidity reports as well as additional reports that are not normally prepared. Reports that are generally prepared during a crisis include but are not limited to the following:

- Levels and trends in uninsured deposit relationships.
- Cash flow projections and run-off reports.
- Reports on performance in relation to liquidity limits and benchmarks
- Funding capacity reports by funding type.
- Certificate of deposit (CD) breakage or early redemption reports.
- Funding source concentration reports.
- Reports on alternative funding sources of incremental liquidity, including standby emergency sources of liquidity.
- Vault cash management reports.
- Intraday settlement and clearing activity reports.
- Daylight overdraft reports.
- Wire transfer activity.

- Information and reports on the stability, pricing, and performance of the markets from which funds would be obtained.

To ensure the effective and timely implementation of the CFP, banks should develop a process for identifying a potential liquidity event before it becomes a crisis. This can be accomplished through the use of early warning indicators and event triggers that are readily observable during the bank's normal reporting process. These should be tailored to the bank's specific liquidity risk profile. For example, a bank should have early warning indicators that signal whether embedded triggers in certain products (i.e., callable public debt, over-the-counter derivatives transactions) are about to be breached, or whether contingent risks are likely to materialize, such as backup lines to off-balance-sheet conduits (i.e., ABCP), which would force a bank to provide additional liquidity support for the product or bring assets back onto the balance sheet. Early recognition of a potential event allows bank management to enhance a bank's readiness as the event actually evolves. Early warning signals may include the following:

- Rapid asset growth funded with volatile liabilities.
- A reluctance of traditional fund providers to continue funding at historic levels.
- Rating agency credit watches for potential downgrades.
- Pending regulatory action (both formal and informal) or CAMELS component or composite rating downgrade(s).
- Significant deterioration in the institution's asset quality.
- Widening of spreads on senior and subordinated debts, credit default swaps, and stock price declines.
- Negative publicity regarding credit quality or reputation.
- Difficulty in accessing long-term debt markets.
- Reluctance of trust managers, money managers, public entities, and credit-sensitive funds providers to place funds.
- Reluctance of broker-dealers to show the institution's name in the market.
- Market rumors or concerns that customers have discussed with the institution's staff.
- Rising funding costs in an otherwise-stable market.
- Increased redemptions of CDs over $250,000 before maturity.
- Counterparty resistance to off-balance-sheet products or increased margin requirements.
- Market reluctance to carry out planned loan sales.
- The elimination of committed credit lines by counterparties.

- Impending triggers in debt issuance and securitization documentation
- Rapidly rising credit spreads or disruptions in the markets from which a bank obtains its funds.

Banks that issue public debt, use warehouse financing, securitize assets, or engage in material over-the-counter derivatives transactions have material exposure to conditions embedded in the contracts. These triggers should also be included in the event-trigger monitoring processes.

Sound CFP planning includes methods for revising both stress scenarios and contingent funding availability to reflect current market conditions and institution-specific circumstances. Often, the reaction of significant funds providers can vary widely and may reflect the institution's unique crisis situation. As conditions and circumstances change, CFP plans should be continually revised to most accurately project the amount of funding needs and availability of primary and contingent sources.

Institutions should test components of their contingency funding plan in order to assess their reliability under times of stress. Identified actions such as loan sales, repurchasing securities, and central bank borrowing should be periodically tested to ensure that they function as envisioned. Larger more complex institutions can benefit from employing simulations to test communications, coordination, and decision-making processes. For example, late-day simulations can point out specific problems, such as difficulties in selling assets or borrowing new funds when the markets are winding down or staff may become inefficient. In the event a bank is experiencing stress, it is important to know that a CFP not only exists but is being acted on.

Internal Controls

An institution's internal controls consist of procedures, approval processes, reconciliations, reviews, and other mechanisms designed to provide reasonable assurance that the institution achieves its objectives for liquidity risk management. Appropriate controls address all aspects of liquidity risk management, including policy adherence, the adequacy of risk identification, the accuracy and appropriateness of risk measurement and reporting, and compliance with applicable laws and regulations. Controls over assumptions and changes to assumptions are critical. Therefore, internal controls should require that assumptions are not changed without clear justification consistent with approved strategies. Documentation for cash flow assumptions should be readily accessible, understandable, and in an auditable format.

Independent reviews of various components of an institution's liquidity risk management processes should be conducted regularly. These reviews should test and document the current measurement processes, evaluate the system's accuracy, and recommend solutions for identified weaknesses. Independent reviews should also assess compliance with policies and procedures. Noncompliance should be reported to the appropriate level of management to ensure that corrective action is taken.

Supplemental Examination Procedures

These examination procedures supplement the core assessment liquidity objectives in the "Community Bank Supervision" booklet and the liquidity standards in the "Large Bank Supervision" booklet. Examiners should begin their liquidity reviews with those core assessment or minimum objectives and steps. The examiners' assessments of risk, the supervisory strategy objectives, and any examination scope memorandums should determine which of this booklet's procedural and validation steps to perform in order to meet examination objectives. Seldom will every objective or step of this booklet's procedures be required to satisfy examination objectives.

These procedures are intended to provide additional guidance in determining the aggregate level of liquidity risk with the goal of determining whether risk is **low, moderate,** or **high.** The procedures are not meant to be performed strictly in the order presented, but should be fit to the bank's or examination's particular circumstances. The liquidity review should be closely coordinated with the reviews of examiners responsible for other areas of the bank (e.g., capital, earnings, credit, sensitivity to market risk, compliance, fiduciary, and information systems). Such coordination can reduce burden on the bank, prevent duplication of examination efforts, and be an effective crosscheck of compliance and process integrity.

Expanded Quantity of Risk Procedures

Objective: To determine the impact of a troubled institution's overall financial condition on the liquidity risk profile.

1.   Review factors that influence credit-sensitive funds providers at the bank level. Consider

- current asset quality and potential deterioration.
- poor earnings performance.
- negative media attention.
- rating agency "watch" or downgrade announcements.
- legal restrictions, such as those on brokered deposits, interbank liabilities, pass-through deposit insurance, Federal Reserve discount window borrowing, and prompt corrective action by regulators.

- whether a waiver from the FDIC for accepting brokered deposits is required, and, if it is, whether it has been obtained and that other legal requirements have been met, including any restrictions on aggregate brokered deposit use.
- characteristics of the bank's customers, such as whether the bank is oriented toward wholesale or retail, the duration of banking relationships, the proportion of customers using more than one product, the customer funds flow cycle, and demographics.
- other economic circumstances in the bank's market or trade area.

Objective: To determine the impact of the bank's organizational structure on the quantity of liquidity risk.

1.   If the bank belongs to a multibank holding company, the primary review of liquidity and funding should be on a consolidated basis.

- Apply the appropriate core and supplemental procedures included in this booklet to your review of the consolidated multi-bank liquidity management system.

2.   Review the parent company's financial condition. Determine

- whether there are short-term liquidity gaps that the parent may have difficulty funding.
- the strength of the parent company's cash and liquid asset positions.
- legal restrictions, such as loans to affiliates (371c), dividend restrictions (12 USC 56 and 60), etc.
- capital needs of affiliate banks that may draw on the resources of the parent or, conversely, affiliate banks with very high capital levels.

3.   Determine the level of risk posed by affiliates. Consider

- any trends in the consolidated liquidity management of cash flows between banks or other affiliates.
- short-term liquidity gaps or other funding or capital needs at an affiliate.
- any surplus liquidity at affiliates.

4.   Review the following indicators that the parent bank or any affiliates are viewed adversely in the market:

- Paying premiums over market (peer) rates on liabilities and capital
- Reduced volume of traditional liability sources
- Reductions in available liability maturities
- Significant liability restructuring, for example, a shift from domestic to foreign funding that is not consistent with strategic plans or objectives
- Political divisiveness (within the bank or holding company) that impedes prudent liquidity practices
- Rating watch or downgrade
- Widening debt spreads relative to bonds of similar credit risk and tenor

Objective: To determine the impact of the use of public funds on the quantity of liquidity risk.

1.   Review public funds and the bank's method of acquiring such funds to determine the profitability, stability, and rate sensitivity of these accounts. Consider

- reasons for the acquisition and use of these funds.
- provider's credit and rate sensitivity.
- potential for purchasing public debt.
- interest rate the bank will pay relative to other funding sources and asset yields.
- pledging requirements and management's controls over collateral availability.
- pricing policies.
- any interest-sensitive deposit products (those with variable rates, floors, or ceilings on interest paid, for example).

Objective: To determine the impact of nontraditional deposit sources on the bank's liquidity profile.

1.   Review deposits gathered by nontraditional means (e.g., broker, Internet listing service, or other deposit-gathering or splitting network). Determine

- the bank's level of reliance on this funding source.
- the stability and rate sensitivity of these deposits.
- management's ability to monitor and control both the inflow and outflow of funds generated via nontraditional methods
- the use of these funds and the bank's ability to deploy them profitably and without undue risk.
- the effectiveness of management reporting and controls over concentrations, collateral requirements, and rollover risk.
- compliance with third-party requirements, including maintaining minimum external and regulatory ratings, and capital adequacy.
- any competitive pressures, economic conditions, or other factors that may affect the gathering and retention of these deposits.

Objective: To determine the impact of securitization activities on the quantity of liquidity risk.

1. Review the bank's asset securitization activities. Examine

    - the role of securitization, if any, in funding activities and plans.
    - securitization performance.
    - securitization trigger reports to determine risk of funding early amortization or termination.
    - the impact of general market or bank-specific circumstances on the acceptance of the bank's securitizations in the marketplace.
    - contingencies, early amortization, or repurchase risk by reviewing securitization agreements.

Objective: As applicable, determine the impact of overdrafts and uncollected funds on the bank's liquidity risk exposure.

1. Cross-reference overdraft and uncollected funds reports to credit line slips of the various loan departments. Examine credit files on significant overdrafts and depositors who frequently draw significant amounts against uncollected funds that were not included in the sample reviewed by the loan portfolio management examiner. Ask management to charge uncollectible overdrafts to the reserve for possible loan losses. Submit a list of overdrafts considered "loss" and the total amounts overdrawn 30 days or more to the examiner assigned loan portfolio management.

2.   Determine whether formal overdraft agreements exist. Obtain the trial balance, or list of agreements, and reconcile it to credit line slips of various loan departments. When formal overdraft agreements are not included in the loan portfolio management examiner's sample, review credit files on significant formal agreements.

Objective: To determine the impact of possible contingent risk related to loan sales and participations on the bank's liquidity risk profile.

1.   Determine, from consultation with the examiners assigned loan portfolio management, that the following schedules were reviewed in the lending departments and that there was no endorsement, guarantee, or repurchase agreement that would constitute a borrowing. Review

     • participations sold.
     • loans sold in full since the preceding examination.

Objective: To determine the reliance on financial market-based funding sources and the risks posed by these activities.

1.   Determine the bank's reliance on products and programs whose funds are obtained from financial market investors or whose underlying collateral is traded through primary or secondary financial market channels (e.g., corporate debt, trust-preferred securities, asset-backed commercial paper conduits, covered bonds, structured investment vehicles, and other market-based asset sales and distribution programs). Review

     • recent issuance volume trends.
     • the performance and quality of underlying assets.
     • changes in the market's acceptance of specific bank issues or issues originated by other market participants and management's efforts to mitigate or address any concerns.
     • changes in the market's appetite for the collateral underlying these programs.
     • trends in interest rates and comparison of spreads to other similar market issuances.
     • management's assessment of the degree of contractual or noncontractual funding support for these facilities that may be

required by the bank under a variety of market and economic conditions.
- the adequacy of the bank's contingency funding and planning for liquidity needs during significant market disruptions or times of stress.

Expanded Quality of Risk Management Procedures

Objective: To determine if the contingency funding plan is commensurate with the risk profile of the institution.

Review the liquidity contingency funding plan (CFP) and the minutes of ALCO meetings and board meetings, and discuss with management the adequacy of the institution's contingent planning processes for liquidity. Determine whether the planning process incorporates

- customization of the CFP to fit the bank's liquidity risk profile.
- identification of potential sources and uses of liquidity under stress events, including all material on- and off-balance-sheet cash flows and their related effects.
- regular use of stress testing for a range of institution-specific and market-wide events across multiple time horizons.
- breadth of potential stress triggers and events and the analyses of various levels of stress to liquidity that can occur under defined scenarios.
- quantitative assessment of short-term and intermediate-term funding needs in stress events.
- the reasonableness of the assumptions used in forecasting potential contingent liquidity needs and the frequency of management's review of these assumptions to ensure they remain valid.
- comprehensiveness in forecasting cash flows under stress conditions, including the incorporation of off-balance-sheet cash flows.
- use of contingent liquidity risk triggers to monitor, on an ongoing basis, the potential for contingent liquidity events.
- assessment of the level of severity, timing, and duration of the stress event.
- consideration of the limitations of payment systems and their operational implications to the bank's ability to access contingent funding.

- operating policies and procedures to be implemented in stress events, including assignment of responsibilities for communicating with various stakeholders.
- prioritization of actions for responding to stress situations.

Objective: To determine whether management's deposit development and retention program is adequate and whether this program is consistent with the overall strategic plan and budget.

1. Determine whether the bank's deposit-marketing strategy is reasonable. Consider

    - whether indications are that the bank's product offerings are responsive to customer needs.
    - current market share and goals for maintaining or increasing market share.
    - the bank's marketing goals and the staff members responsible for meeting those goals.
    - the bank's anticipated deposit structure and interest costs of such a structure.
    - a periodic comparison of performance with projections, including periodic formal or informal reports to management on results and the accuracy of cost projections.
    - consistency of the bank's overall strategic plan with its budget.

Objective: To assess the adequacy of liquidity risk management information systems.

1. Review liquidity risk management policies, procedures, and reports. Then discuss with management the frequency and comprehensiveness of liquidity risk reporting for various levels of management responsible for monitoring and managing liquidity risk. Considerations should include the following:

    - Management's need to receive reports that
        - determine compliance with limits and controls.
        - evaluate the results of past strategies.
        - assess the potential risks and returns of proposed strategies.
        - identify the major changes in a bank's liquidity risk profile.

- consolidate the liquidity position for the bank and all significant subsidiaries.

- The need for the reporting system to be flexible enough to
  - quickly collect and edit data, summarize results, and adapt to changing circumstances or issues.
  - increase the frequency of preparation as conditions deteriorate or the need arises.

- The need for reports to focus properly on monitoring liquidity and supporting decision making. Such reports often help bank management to monitor
  - sources and uses of funds, facilitating the evaluation of trends and structural balance-sheet changes.
  - contingency funding plans.
  - projected cash flow or maturity gaps, identifying potential future liquidity needs. Reports should show projections using both contractual maturities (original maturity dates) and behavioral maturities (maturities attributable to the expected behaviors of customers).
  - consolidated large funds providers, identifying customer concentrations. Reports should identify and aggregate major liability instruments used by large customers in the consolidated bank.
  - the cost of funds from all significant funding sources, enabling management to do a quick cost comparison.

Objective: To assess the adequacy of internal controls surrounding the liquidity risk management process.

1. Determine whether the board and senior management have established clear lines of authority and responsibility for monitoring adherence to policies, procedures, and limits. Review policies, procedures, and reports to ascertain whether the institution's

    - measurement system adequately captures and quantifies risk.
    - limits are appropriately defined, communicated to management, and routinely compared to actual liquidity measures.

2.   Determine whether internal controls and information systems are adequately tested and reviewed by ascertaining whether the institution's

- risk measurement tools are accurate, independent, and reliable.
- frequency of testing of controls is adequate given the level of risk and sophistication of risk management decisions.
- reports provide relevant information, including comments on major changes in risk profiles.

3.   Determine whether the liquidity management function is audited internally, or externally, or whether it is evaluated by the risk management function. Also ascertain whether the audit or evaluation is independent and of sufficient scope by determining

- whether audit findings and management responses to those findings are fully documented and tracked for adequate follow-up.
- whether line management is held accountable for unsatisfactory or ineffective follow-up.
- whether risk managers give identified material weaknesses appropriate and timely attention.
- whether actions taken by management to deal with material weaknesses have been verified and reviewed for objectivity and adequacy by senior management or the board.
- that the board and senior management have established adequate procedures for ensuring compliance with applicable laws and regulations.

Objective: To determine the adequacy of procedures and controls over wholesale funding activities.

1.   Determine whether the bank maintains subsidiary records for each type of borrowing, including proper identification of the obligee.

2.   Determine whether corporate borrowing resolutions are properly prepared as required by creditors and whether copies are on file for reviewing personnel.

3.   Determine whether any area has inadequate supervision or poses risk.

4. Determine whether subsidiary records are reconciled with the general ledger accounts at an interval consistent with borrowing activity, and that reconciling items are investigated by persons who do not also

   - handle cash.
   - prepare or post to the subsidiary records.

5. Determine whether individual interest computations are checked by persons who do not have access to cash.

6. Determine whether an overall test of the total interest paid is made by persons who do not have access to cash.

7. Determine whether payees on the checks are matched to related records of debt, note, or debenture owners.

Objective: To determine compliance with the terms of wholesale funding agreements.

1. If the bank engages in any form of wholesale funding that requires written agreement(s),

   - determine whether the bank is in compliance with those terms.
   - review terms of past and present borrowing agreements for indications of a deteriorating credit position by noting
     - recent substantive changes in borrowing agreements.
     - increases in collateral to support borrowing transactions.
     - a general shortening of maturities.
     - interest rates exceeding prevailing market rates.
     - frequent changes in lenders.
     - large fees paid to money brokers.

Objective: To assess the adequacy of controls over liquidity exposure associated with foreign currency.

1. Determine whether the bank has a measurement, monitoring, and control system for its liquidity positions in the major currencies in which it is active.

2. Determine whether the bank has undertaken a separate analysis of its strategy for each currency individually.

3. Determine whether the bank has appropriately defined and regularly reviewed limits on the size of its cash flow mismatches over specified time horizons for foreign currencies **in aggregate** and **for each significant individual currency** in which the bank operates.

Objective: To determine whether the bank's public disclosure (e.g., quarterly or annual public financial statements) practices are adequate and do not adversely affect the bank's liquidity position.

1. Determine whether the bank has a process in place that ensures there is an adequate level of disclosure of information about the bank in order to manage public perception of the organization and its soundness.

2. Determine whether other factors have a material effect on liquidity risk exposure. Consider the potential impact of institutional trends such as asset growth, asset quality, earnings trends, and market risk exposures (both interest-rate risk in the banking book and trading book exposures). Review also business-line operational considerations and the potential for legal and reputation risk.

Objective: To determine whether processes for managing risk exposures to correspondents and processes for complying with Regulation F (12 CFR 206, "Limitations on Interbank Liabilities")[12] and OCC Bulletin 2010-16, "Correspondent Concentration Risks" are adequate.

1. Review OCC and internal bank reports to identify any undue concentration of risk created by interbank credit exposure. Consider

   - exposures greater than 25 percent of capital.
   - liability funding concentrations with significant counterparties.
   - exposures as a percentage of total assets.

---

[12] The purpose of this regulation is to limit the risks that the failure of a depository institution (foreign or domestic) would pose to insured depository institutions. "Exposure" includes all types of banking transactions that create a risk of nonpayment or delayed payment between institutions. "Correspondent" excludes commonly controlled institutions.

- interbank assets placed with correspondents whose financial condition is deteriorating.

2. Request bank files relating to exposures to correspondents, as defined in the "Prudential Standards" section of Regulation F (Section 206.3), and evaluate
   - documentation demonstrating that the bank has periodically reviewed the financial condition of all correspondents to which it has significant exposure. The documentation should address the levels of the correspondent's capital, nonaccrual and past-due loans and leases, earnings, and other matters pertinent to its financial condition.
   - information from the bank indicating the levels of exposures to correspondents as measured by its internal control systems. (For smaller banks this information may include correspondent statements and a list of securities held in safekeeping for the bank by the correspondent.)

3. Review the information obtained in the preceding step for reasonableness based on discussions with examiners of other banking activities and review of their findings. Consider

   - asset management
   - computer services
   - payment systems and funds transfer activities
   - private placements
   - international department activities
   - off-balance-sheet products (including derivatives)

4. Request a list of all correspondents to which the bank regularly has credit exposure, as defined in the "Credit Exposure" section of Regulation F (Section 206.4), equal to more than 25 percent of capital for a specified length of time. Review the bank's files to determine whether

   - the capital levels of correspondents are monitored quarterly.
   - those institutions are adequately capitalized as defined by Regulation F.
   - credit exposure to correspondents at risk of dropping below the adequately capitalized level could be reduced to an amount equal to 25 percent of capital or less in a timely manner.

5. Determine whether the bank maintains accounts at foreign institutions or whether foreign institutions maintain accounts at the bank. If so, determine whether the compliance examination tested for compliance with 12 CFR 21.21 (Bank Secrecy Act), 31 CFR 103 (Financial Record Keeping and Reporting of Currency and Foreign Transactions), and policies that address the collection of customer background information.

6. Determine whether the bank has significant exposure to a correspondent because of transaction risks, such as extensive reliance on a correspondent for data processing. If so, determine whether the bank has addressed those risks.

7. Confirm that the bank's process for monitoring significant exposure (especially for correspondents that are less than adequately capitalized or financially deteriorating) is appropriate. Consider

   - type and volatility of exposure.
   - extent to which the exposure approaches the bank's internal limits.
   - condition of the correspondent. Also consider
     - capital.
     - nonaccrual and past-due loans and leases.
     - earnings.
     - other relevant factors.

8. For credit exposure to correspondents that are adequately capitalized, review the bank's monitoring process to determine whether

   - management obtains quarterly information to determine its correspondent's capital levels.
   - management monitors overnight credit exposure.
   - the monitoring frequency is adequate.

9. Determine how often the bank reviews the financial condition of institutions to which it has very large or long-term exposure and how often it reviews institutions whose financial condition is deteriorating.

10. Determine whether the frequency of these reviews is adequate for the level of exposure and financial condition of the correspondent.

11. Determine whether the bank

- relies on another party (such as its holding company, a bank rating agency, or another correspondent) to provide financial analysis of a correspondent. If so, verify that the bank's board of directors reviewed and approved the assessment criteria used by that party.
- relies on another party to select or monitor its correspondents. If so, verify that the bank's board of directors reviewed and approved the selection criteria used.
- relies on a correspondent to choose other correspondents to whom the bank lends federal funds. If so, verify that the bank's board of directors reviewed and approved the selection criteria used.
- evaluates the creditworthiness of each correspondent and the appropriate level of exposure to a correspondent whose financial condition is deteriorating.

Objective: To determine compliance with applicable laws and regulations regarding deposit accounts. **(If there is a concurrent consumer compliance examination, coordinate with the examiner assigned compliance with deposit regulations when carrying out procedures.)**

1. **12 USC 90, Depositaries of Public Moneys and Financial Agents of Government.** Select several public deposit accounts along with pledging records and determine compliance.

2. **12 USC 501 and 18 USC 1004, Certification of Checks.** Select several certified checks and compare the date and amount of certification to similarly dated uncollected funds and overdraft reports to determine whether checks were certified against collected funds.

3. **12 CFR 7.4002, Charges by Banks.** Determine whether the bank's service charges and fees are reasonable.

4. **12 CFR 7.4002, Service Charges on Dormant Accounts.** Determine whether any complaints relating to the bank's dormant account practices have been filed, whether the complaints reflect a pattern of practices inconsistent with the bank's deposit contracts, whether service charges on several additional dormant accounts selected are consistent with deposit contracts, and whether the board has reviewed the bank's service charges on dormant accounts and has confirmed for the record that the charges are reasonable.

5.   **12 CFR 337.6, Brokered Deposits.** If the bank is below the "well-capitalized" capital category, review the bank's policies and practices to ensure compliance.

6.   Review the bank for compliance with the regulation on treasury tax and loan (TT&L) accounts (31 CFR 203.9 and 203.10).

   - Do transfers from the remittance option account to the Federal Reserve Bank occur the next business day after deposit?
   - Is the remittance option included in the computation of reserve requirements?
   - When the note option is used, do transfers from the TT&L demand deposit account occur the next business day after deposit?

7.   **31 CFR 210, Federal Recurring Payments Through Financial Institutions.** Determine that for federal recurring payments other than by check, affected employees are familiar with the regulation's requirements. Determine that the bank executes the "standard authorization form" for customer accounts that will receive recurring payments (deposits) from the federal government. Determine that deposits are credited to the designated account and that funds are made available for withdrawal not later than the opening of business on the deposit date. Verify that deposits that cannot be posted are returned promptly to the government.

8.   **Uniform Commercial Code (UCC) 4-107, 211, 212, 301, and 302, Banking Hours and Processing of Demand Items.** Determine the bank's established cutoff hour for processing items on the next banking day.[13] If the established cutoff is before 2 p.m., determine whether items received after the cutoff but before 2 p.m. are processed as having been received on the same banking day, as required by UCC 4-107. Failure to process items received before 2 p.m. **may** result in civil liability for items subsequently dishonored. If the bank is open for business on Saturday, determine the established cutoff hour for processing items on the next banking day. If the established cutoff is before 2 p.m., determine whether items received after the cutoff but before 2 p.m. are processed as having been received on Saturday, as

---

[13] A "banking day" is defined as a day during which a bank is open to the public for carrying on substantially all of its banking functions. A day on which the bank did no more than receive deposits and cash checks is not a banking day. To be a banking day, the bookkeeping and loan departments must be operating, as well as a teller's window.

required by UCC 4-107. Failure to process them as of Saturday **may** expose the bank to civil liability under UCC 4-211, 212, 301, and 302 for demand items that are subsequently dishonored.

9. **Local escheat laws.** Determine that the bank adheres to the local escheat laws on any form of dormant deposits.

Conclude the Liquidity Review

Objective: To prepare written conclusions and supporting comments and to communicate findings to management. Review findings with the EIC before discussing them with management.

1. Determine the CAMELS component rating for liquidity.[14] Consider

    - whether management is able to properly measure, monitor, and control the institution's liquidity position, including whether funds management strategies, liquidity policies, management information systems, and contingency funding plans are effective.
    - the adequacy of liquidity sources in light of present and future needs and the ability of the institution to remain liquid without compromising its operations or condition. Capital adequacy, asset quality, earnings stability, and management stability are primary considerations.
    - whether sufficient assets are readily convertible to cash without undue loss.
    - access to money markets and other sources of funding.
    - the level of diversification of funding sources, both on and off balance sheet.
    - how much the bank relies on short-term, credit-sensitive sources of funds, including borrowings and brokered deposits, to fund longer-term assets.
    - the trend and stability of deposits.
    - the ability to securitize and sell certain pools of assets.

2. Determine assessments of the quantity of liquidity risk, quality of risk management, and the aggregate level and direction of risk.

---

[14] Examiner should refer to the "Bank Supervision Process" booklet for the CAMELS component rating definition for liquidity.

- Determine the quantity of liquidity risk (**low, moderate, high**). Consider
  - availability and cost effectiveness of funding sources.
  - diversification of funding sources.
  - availability and cost effectiveness of market alternatives for funding.
  - capacity to augment liquidity through asset sales or securitizations, including market accessibility.
  - level of and trends in reliance on wholesale funding sources.
  - volume of wholesale liabilities with embedded options.
  - vulnerability to funding difficulties arising from material adverse changes to market perception.
  - support provided by the parent company.
  - earnings and capital exposure to liquidity risk.

- Determine the quality of liquidity risk management (**strong, satisfactory, weak**). Consider
  - appropriateness and effectiveness of policies, procedures, and limits.
  - effectiveness of board or ALCO supervision.
  - effectiveness of the liquidity risk management process in identifying, measuring, monitoring, and controlling risk.
  - level of sophistication necessary to effectively manage liquidity.
  - management's knowledge and understanding of the bank's liquidity risk exposure.
  - adequacy of contingency funding plans, including whether it is current, reasonably addresses most relevant issues, and provides an adequate level of detail and breadth for scenario analyses.
  - adequacy, accuracy, and timeliness of MIS, including whether its focus is on significant liquidity risk exposures.

- Determine the aggregate level of liquidity risk (**low, moderate, high**). Consider
  - the assessment of the quality of risk management in relation to the level of liquidity risk exposure.

- Determine the direction of risk (**decreasing, stable, increasing**). Consider
  - potential for changes in the risk profile due to new or planned activities.

  – trends in reliance on or changes in wholesale funding.
  – potential impact of local, regional, and national markets on future liquidity levels.
  – ability of management to effectively and efficiently resolve a potential adverse liquidity scenario.

3. Determine whether performing the foregoing procedures has changed assessments of any associated risks. Consider the quantity of risk, the quality of management, the direction of risk, and the amount of supervisory concern (aggregate risk). Examiners should consult the OCC's guidance on assessing risks, either the guidance for large banks or that for community banks, as appropriate. Consider the risk categories of compliance, credit, interest rate, liquidity, price, reputation, strategic, and operational.

For a bank with a liquidity component rating of 1 or 2:

4. Provide the EIC with a conclusion supporting the following:

- CAMELS component rating
- Risk assessments

For a bank with a liquidity component rating of 3 or worse:

5. Provide a detailed conclusion comment to the EIC that

- addresses deficiencies.
- identifies the root causes of deficiencies noted.
- discusses the reasons for the less-than-satisfactory performance.
- addresses management's ability to correct the deficiencies noted.
- addresses risk assessments.

6. Develop, in consultation with the EIC, a supervisory strategy to address the bank's weaknesses and discuss the strategy with the appropriate supervisory office or manager.

For all banks, regardless of rating:

7. Determine, in consultation with the EIC, whether any issues identified are significant enough to merit bringing them to the board's attention in

the report of examination (ROE). If so, prepare items for inclusion in the section of the ROE on matter(s) requiring attention (MRA).

- MRAs should cover practices that
  - Deviate from sound governance, internal controls, and risk management principles which may adversely impact the bank's earnings or capital, risk profile, or reputation, if not addressed; or
  - Result in substantive noncompliance with laws and regulations, internal policies or processes, OCC supervisory guidance, or conditions imposed in writing in connection with the approval of any application or other request by a bank

- MRAs should discuss
  - concern(s)
  - causes(s) of the problem.
  - consequence(s) of inaction.
  - corrective action(s).
  - commitment(s): time frame and person(s) responsible for corrective action(s).

8. Discuss findings with management, including conclusions regarding applicable risks. Consider

- adequacy of liquidity sources in light of present and future needs.
- ability of the institution to meet liquidity needs without adversely affecting its operations or condition.
- compliance with policy.
- degree of reliance on credit-sensitive funding sources.
- ability of management to identify, measure, monitor, and control the institution's liquidity position.

9. Prepare a liquidity comment for inclusion in the report of examination.

10. Prepare a memorandum or update the work program with any information that will facilitate future examinations.

11. Update the OCC database and any applicable risk profile, report-of-examination schedules or tables.

12. Organize and reference work papers in accordance with OCC policy.

Appendix A: Brokered Deposit Use and Restrictions
(Law: 12 USC 1831f; Regulation: 12 CFR 337.6)

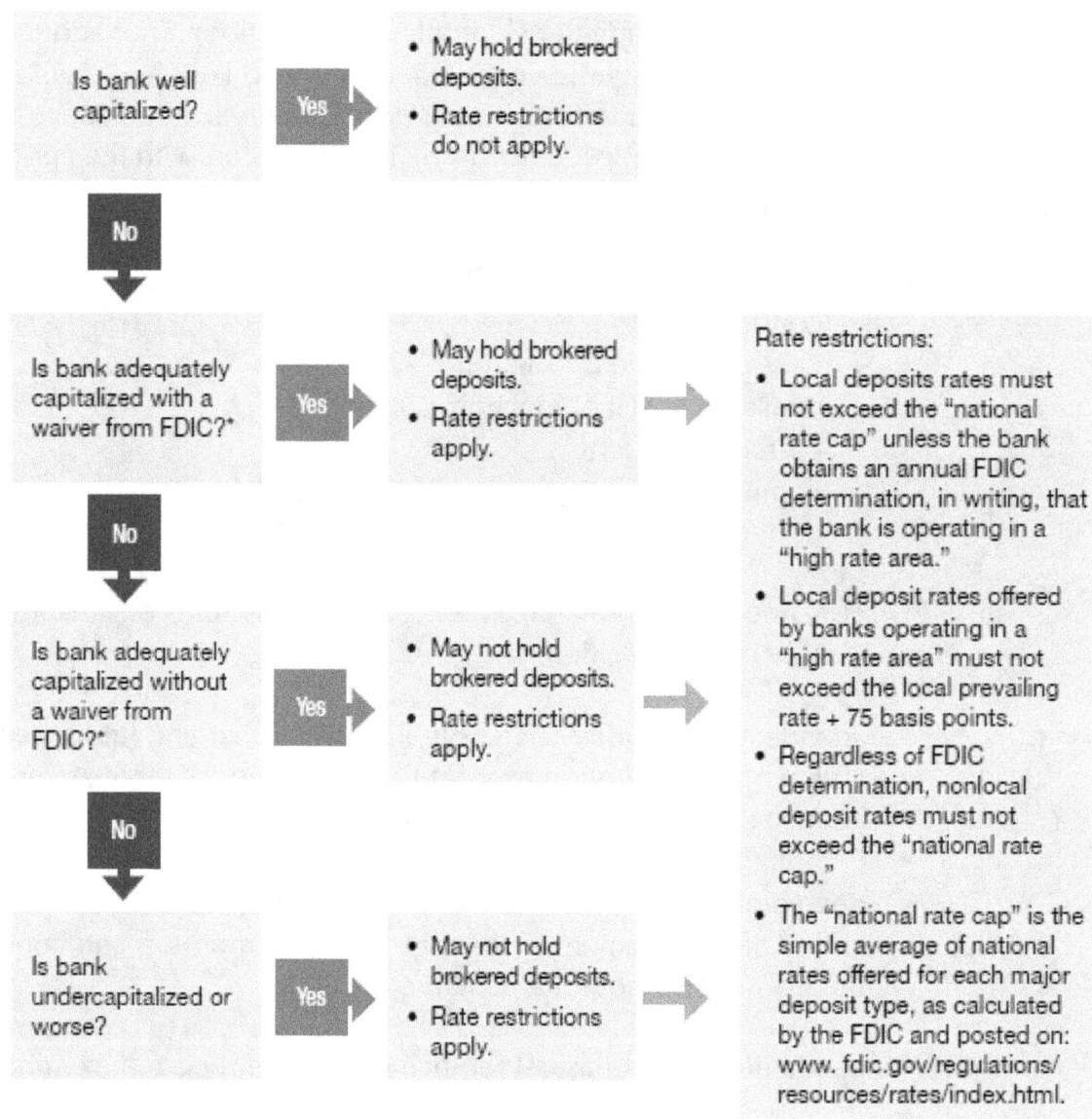

* Includes banks that are reclassified "adequately capitalized" for being subject to a capital maintenance provision within a Formal Agreement, Cease and Desist Order, Capital Directive, Prompt Corrective Action Directive, or other formal agreement issued by a federal regulator. A Board Resolution, Memorandum of Understanding, Individual Minimum Capital Ratio, or other informal agreement does not reclassify a well-capitalized bank.

Appendix B: Example—National Bank
Projected Sources and Uses Statement
As of September 30, 20XX
Scenario 1

Primary liquidity position	Actual Prior month	Six months projected 1st month	2nd month	3rd month	4th month	5th month	6th month
Fed funds position (purchased or sold) (FFP or FFS)	10	8	5	4	2	(1)	(4)
Sources of funds							
Loans reductions	1	3	5	13	7	8	3
Nonmaturity deposit growth	2	1	1	2	1	0	2
Time deposit growth	1	1	2	0	0	3	2
Borrowing growth	0	0	0	0	0	0	0
Investment maturities	2	2	3	2	0	0	4
Change in equity	0	0	0	1	0	0	1
Other (including off-balance-sheet)	0	0	0	0	0	0	0
A. Total sources of funds	**16**	**15**	**16**	**22**	**10**	**10**	**8**
Uses of funds							
Loan growth/funded commitments	2	3	6	14	9	10	5
Nonmaturity deposit reductions	1	2	0	1	1	0	0
Time deposit reduction	2	1	1	0	0	1	1
Brokered CDs maturing	1	0	1	0	0	0	0
Investment purchases	2	2	2	2	0	1	3
Borrowing reduction	0	2	2	0	1	2	0
Other (including off-balance-sheet)	0	0	0	0	0	0	0
B. Total uses of funds	**8**	**10**	**12**	**20**	**11**	**14**	**9**
C. Projected cash flow* (A − B)	**8**	**5**	**4**	**2**	**(1)**	**(4)**	**(1)**
Liquidity coverage ratio (B/C)	**2.00**	**1.50**	**1.33**	**1.10**	**0.91**	**0.71**	**0.89**

Secondary liquidity sources	Actual	Six months projected					
	Prior month	1st month	2nd month	3rd month	4th month	5th month	6th month
Unpledged investments (Available for repo / FHLB advance collateral)	30	30	30	30	30	30	30
Unsecured Fed funds lines	5	5	5	5	5	5	5
Brokered CD subject to policy limits	10	10	11	12	12	12	12
FHLB and other borrowing lines	20	20	20	20	20	20	20
Loans available to securitize/sell	10	10	10	10	10	10	10
D. Total secondary sources	75	75	76	77	77	77	77
Capacity coverage ratio (C/D) (secondary sources to projected negative cash flow)	N/A	N/A	N/A	N/A	77	19	77
Total liquidity before Fed discount window borrowing (C + D)	83	80	80	79	76	73	76
Policy limit**	XX	XX	XX	XX	XX	XX	XX
Within policy limits	Yes	Yes	Yes	Yes	Yes	No	Yes

Note: This is a simple example. Banks should tailor the format, level of detail, scenarios, and time periods to best meet their needs. Multiple scenarios may be generated for projected business strategies, rate environments, local and national economic conditions, or cash flow uncertainties.

*   This report assumes that monthly projected cash flows roll into FFS or are funded by FFP.

**   Policy limits should be tailored to the nature and extent of the bank's liquidity risk exposure (e.g., volatile funding dependence, acceptable coverage of potential volatile funding, available capacity to projected cash flow). Examples of volatile funding may include brokered deposits, borrowing lines, uninsured deposits.

Appendix C: Example—National Bank
Liquidity Gap Report
12 Months Projected
As of September 30, 20XX

Balance sheet	Beg B/S	Over-night	Month 1	Month 2	Month 3	Month 4	Month 5	Month 6	Month 7	Month 8	Month 9	Month 10	Month 11	Month 12	0–12 mos.	> 12 mos.
Assets																
Fed funds sold (FFS)	**10**	**10**	**0**	**0**	**0**	**0**	**0**	**0**	**0**	**0**	**0**	**0**	**0**	**0**	**10**	**0**
Investment portfolio																
MBS	20	0	0	1	1	0	0	1	0	1	1	0	0	0	5	15
Agency callable	10	0	0	1	0	0	0	0	1	0	2	0	0	0	4	6
CMOs	5	0	1	0	0	0	0	0	1	0	0	0	0	0	2	3
Corporate fixed	5	0	0	0	0	0	0	1	0	0	0	0	0	0	1	4
Municipal bonds fixed	10	0	0	0	1	0	0	1	0	0	0	0	0	1	3	7
Investment portfolio total	**60**	**10**	**1**	**2**	**2**	**0**	**0**	**3**	**2**	**1**	**3**	**0**	**0**	**1**	**25**	**35**
Loan portfolio																
C&I	30	0	1	2	2	2	2	2	2	0	0	0	2	1	16	14
Commercial mortgage	40	0	1	1	1	2	2	1	0	0	0	3	1	1	13	27
Credit card loans	10	0	0	0	10	0	0	0	0	0	0	0	0	0	10	0
Residential	40	0	1	1	1	2	3	0	1	1	1	2	1	0	14	26
Home equity loans	20	0	0	0	3	0	0	1	0	0	1	0	0	0	5	15
Loan portfolio total	**140**	**0**	**3**	**4**	**17**	**6**	**7**	**4**	**3**	**1**	**2**	**5**	**4**	**2**	**58**	**82**
Total assets	**200**	**10**	**4**	**6**	**19**	**6**	**7**	**7**	**5**	**2**	**5**	**5**	**4**	**3**	**83**	**117**

Balance sheet	Beg B/S	Over-night	Month 1	Month 2	Month 3	Month 4	Month 5	Month 6	Month 7	Month 8	Month 9	Month 10	Month 11	Month 12	0–12 mos.	> 12 mos.
Liabilities																
Retail funding																
DDA	30	0	1	1	1	0	0	1	0	0	1	0	0	1	6	24
MMDA	40	5	0	0	17	0	0	0	0	0	0	0	0	0	22	18
NOW	20	0	2	1	2	0	0	2	0	0	2	0	0	2	11	9
CDs	40	0	2	2	1	3	3	0	1	2	3	1	3	1	22	18
Savings	20	0	1	1	1	0	0	0	0	0	1	1	1	0	6	14
Retail funding total	**150**	**5**	**6**	**5**	**22**	**3**	**3**	**3**	**1**	**2**	**7**	**2**	**4**	**4**	**67**	**83**
Wholesale funding																
Fed funds purchased/ Overnight advances	10	10	0	0	0	0	0	0	0	0	0	0	0	0	0	10
Term advance	20	0	0	5	0	0	0	0	0	0	5	0	0	0	10	10
Wholesale funding total	**30**	**10**	**0**	**5**	**0**	**0**	**0**	**0**	**0**	**0**	**5**	**0**	**0**	**0**	**20**	**10**
Total liabilities	180	25	6	10	22	3	3	3	1	2	17	2	4	4	30	150
Equity	20	0	0	0	0	0	0	0	0	0	0	0	0	0	0	20
Total liabilities & equity	**200**	**25**	**6**	**10**	**22**	**3**	**3**	**3**	**1**	**2**	**17**	**2**	**4**	**4**	**97**	**103**
Net period gap (deficit)		(15)	(2)	(4)	(3)	3	4	4	4	0	(12)	3	0	(1)		
Liquidity gap % assets		(0.08)	(0.20)	(1.00)	(0.50)	0.16	0.67	0.57	0.57	0.00	(6.00)	0.60	0.00	(0.25)		
Cumulative gap		(15)	(17)	(21)	(24)	(21)	(17)	(13)	(9)	(9)	(21)	(18)	(18)	(19)		
Cumulative liquidity gap % assets		-7.5%	-8.5%	-10.5%	-12.0%	-10.5%	-8.5%	-6.5%	-4.5%	-4.5%	-10.5%	-9.0%	-9.0%	-9.5%		
Policy limit		XX	XX	XX	XX	XX	XX	XX	XX	XX	XX	XX	XX	XX		
Policy limit compliance		Yes	Yes	Yes	No	Yes	Yes	Yes	Yes	Yes	Yes	Yes	Yes	Yes		

Note: This is a simple example. Banks should tailor the format, level of account detail, scenarios, and extent of time periods included to best meet their needs.

- This report reflects maturities and expected nonmaturity deposit run-off.
- To improve accuracy, banks should adjust cash flows for repayment and prepayments and nonmaturity behavioral assumptions.
- This report should NOT reflect asset and liability repricing.

Appendix D: Examples of Liquidity Stress Events, Triggers, and Monitoring Items or Reports

Stress event	Warning trigger(s)	Possible monitoring items or reports
Actual or threatened watch or downgrade to an external credit rating	Rating agency credit watch for potential downgrades; widening credit spreads; rapid decline in stock price	Market watch or rating agency reports; credit spreads stock performance
Actual or anticipated changes in senior or short-term debt ratings	Rating agency downgrades; widening credit spreads; rapid decline in stock price	Debt spreads; stock performance
Significant asset quality deterioration	Deteriorating trend in loan performance, classified loans, nonperforming, and past-due loans	Problem loan trends report; volume and trends in loan sales
Decline in the institution's composite CAMELS rating	Decline in one or more component rating; adverse financial or operational performance; noncompliance with law or regulation	Reports of Examination; violations of law or regulation; trends in matters requiring attention; risk assessments
A prompt corrective action capital downgrade	Decline in regulatory capital levels; change in prompt corrective action category	Capital adequacy report; bank growth; earnings performance
High and consistent operating losses	Significant decline in earnings performance	Overhead trends report; margin and profitability trends
Negative news coverage	Internal issues that could lead to negative news coverage; market rumors or concerns that customers have discussed with staff	Local and regional press releases or news articles; consumer advocacy attention or complaints
Rising reputation risks	Increasing compliance, transaction risk; violations of law that could result in reimbursement	Compliance audit reports; customer complaints file; consumer advocacy attention or complaints
Adverse changes in the costs of significant funding vehicles	Over-reliance on or concentration in traditionally high-cost funding; significant increases in funding costs	Funding source concentration report; funding capacity reports by funding type; trends in cost of funds by type
Inability to access long-term debt	Difficulty in obtaining long-term debt; widening spreads; increased collateral requirements	Reports on alternative funding sources of incremental liquidity including standby emergency sources; credit spreads; liquid assets to pledged assets report
Loss of name acceptance in the credit markets	Reluctance of broker-dealers to show the institution's name in the market	Market watch or rating agency reports; credit spreads; stock performance
Deposit run; rapid redemption of CDs	Increased early redemption of jumbo CDs; significant declines in overall deposits	CD breakage or early redemption report; cash flow projections and run-off reports; vault cash management reports
Inability to access funding lines	Elimination of committed credit lines by counterparties	Collateral management reports; credit spreads; daylight overdrafts and wire transfer activity reports

Stress event	Warning trigger(s)	Possible monitoring items or reports
Inability to securitize assets	Additional or more stringent requirements for securitization documentation or debt issuance; counterparty resistance of off-balance sheet products or increased margin requirements	Put back or exception reports; securitization performance reports; underwriting standards
Inability to sell assets	Increasing spreads on assets; deterioration in asset market values	Asset spreads; pricing trend analysis; asset impairment reports
Public funds withdrawn; Fed funds or FHLB lines frozen	Reluctance of trust managers, money managers, public entities and credit sensitive funds providers to place funds	Contingent funding availability reports; deposit trends; pledging and safekeeping reports
Significant uncontrolled growth outstripping capital and funding	Rapid growth or acquisition; increasing line draws or usage by large local or regional company	Budget variance, operating plan, strategic plan; loan growth analysis by sector, office, officer, or industry; unfunded commitments or draw schedule

Note: This is not a comprehensive list. Liquidity stress events, triggers, and monitoring items and reports should be developed that best reflect banks' funding activities and structure. In addition to banks' specific stress events, banks should identify potential external events that could create a liquidity crisis, including natural disasters and the affect of severe payment systems and capital markets disruption.

Appendix E: Example—National Bank
Liquidity Contingency Funding Scenarios
Time Period: Three Months
As of September 30, 20XX

Primary liquidity position	Actual	Moderate	Severe	Crisis	Comments on assumptions
Fed funds (purchased or sold)	**10**	**1**	**14**	**10**	
Sources of funds					
Loans reductions	1	0	0	0	Deterioration in local or national economic conditions
Nonmaturity deposit growth	2	5	2	0	Accelerated gathering until bank's condition affects efforts
Time deposit growth	1	10	0	0	Accelerated gathering until bank's condition affects efforts
Borrowing growth	0	5	20	5	Increased securitized borrowings as conditions deteriorate
Investment maturities	2	2	2	2	
Change in equity	0	-1	-2	-10	Impact of increasing funding costs and deteriorating earnings performance
Other sources (including off bal. sheet)	0	0	0	0	
A. Total sources of funds	**16**	**22**	**36**	**7**	
Uses of funds					
Loan growth	2	2	1	0	Loan fundings decline as financial condition or ability to fund deteriorates
Nonmaturity deposit reductions	1	1	2	2	Normal and customary; reaction to stress scenarios captured in "Additional Funding Requirements"
Time deposit reduction	2	2	3	3	Normal maturity of insured CDs
Brokered CDs maturing	1	1	1	1	Normal maturity of brokered CDs
Investment increases	2	0	0	0	Inability to acquire new assets
Borrowing reduction	0	0	0	0	Possible bank negotiations with counterparties to alter terms or lengthen advances
Other	0	0	0	0	
B. Total uses of funds	**8**	**6**	**7**	**6**	
C. Fed funds (period end) (A – B)	**8**	**16**	**29**	**1**	Initial build-up of liquidity, then resulting decline as scenario worsens

63

Secondary liquidity position	Actual	Moderate	Severe	Crisis	Comments on assumptions
Additional funding requirements					
Reduction in DDA, NOW, MMDA, savings	0	3	10	20	Retail customer desire to withdraw funds because of deteriorating financial condition or negative press
Reduction in gov't. NOW	0	2	4	5	Municipalities unwillingness to place funds or lack of collateral
Reduction in time	0	3	10	20	Customer concern with bank condition
Reduction in repos, TT&L	0	2	10	15	Customer or counterparty concern with bank condition
D. Total contingent uses	**0**	**10**	**34**	**60**	
Additional funding sources					
Unpledged investments	30	30	20	5	Sale or repo activity
Unsecured Fed funds lines	5	5	0	0	Initial build up then inability to attract unsecured funds
Brokered CDs potential within policy and regulatory parameters	10	10	10	0	FDIC or prompt corrective action restriction on brokered deposits
FHLB and other borrowing lines	20	20	10	0	Reflect loss of collateral, increased hair cuts, and elimination or freezing of lines
Loans available to securitize or sell	20	20	15	0	Initial funding source, then lack of secondary market acceptance
E. Total secondary sources	**85**	**85**	**55**	**5**	
Total liquidity before Fed discount window borrowing (C – D + E)	**93**	**91**	**50**	**-54**	Determine access to Fed window depending on establishment of line, primary or secondary program status, daylight overdraft status, and extent of pledgeable assets.
Policy target *	XX	XX	XX	XX	Establish and tailor policy limit(s) based upon liquidity risk exposure
Within policy parameters	Yes	Yes	Yes	No	***Board of directors and senior management. should develop strategy to address out-of-policy situation***

Note: This is a simple example. Banks should tailor the format, level of account detail, scenarios, and extent of time periods included to best meet their needs.

* Contingency scenarios and policy parameters should be developed and customized to reflect the bank's liquidity risk exposure. Scenarios should reflect continuing deteriorating liquidity position and employ meaningful assumptions regarding potential fund outflows.

Appendix F: Example—National Bank
Problem Bank—Balance Sheet Trend Report
September 30, 20XX

Reported in (000s)

Time horizon	Period -5	Period -4	Period -3	Period -2	Period -1	Current period	Period +1	Period +2	Period +3	Period +4	Period +5
Balance sheet											
Cash & due from	0	0	0	0	0	0	0	0	0	0	0
FFS	0	0	0	0	0	0	0	0	0	0	0
Securities	0	0	0	0	0	0	0	0	0	0	0
Loans	0	0	0	0	0	0	0	0	0	0	0
ALLL	0	0	0	0	0	0	0	0	0	0	0
Other assets (detail)	0	0	0	0	0	0	0	0	0	0	0
Total assets	**0**	**0**	**0**	**0**	**0**	**0**	**0**	**0**	**0**	**0**	**0**
DDAs	0	0	0	0	0	0	0	0	0	0	0
MMDAs/NOW	0	0	0	0	0	0	0	0	0	0	0
Savings	0	0	0	0	0	0	0	0	0	0	0
CDs	0	0	0	0	0	0	0	0	0	0	0
Other (detail)	0	0	0	0	0	0	0	0	0	0	0
Total deposits	**0**	**0**	**0**	**0**	**0**	**0**	**0**	**0**	**0**	**0**	**0**
FFPs & repos	0	0	0	0	0	0	0	0	0	0	0
FHLB	0	0	0	0	0	0	0	0	0	0	0
Other (detail)	0	0	0	0	0	0	0	0	0	0	0
Total other liabilities	**0**	**0**	**0**	**0**	**0**	**0**	**0**	**0**	**0**	**0**	**0**
Total liabilities	**0**	**0**	**0**	**0**	**0**	**0**	**0**	**0**	**0**	**0**	**0**

Comments and assumptions:

Appendix G: Example—National Bank
Problem Bank—Summary of Available Liquidity Report
September 30, 20XX

Reported in (000s)

Time horizon	Period − 5	Period − 4	Period − 3	Period − 2	Period − 1	Current period	Period + 1	Period + 2	Period + 3	Period + 4	Period + 5
Summary of available liquidity											
Cash & due from (net of operating requirements)	0	0	0	0	0	0	0	0	0	0	0
Fed funds sold	0	0	0	0	0	0	0	0	0	0	0
Repos (sold)	0	0	0	0	0	0	0	0	0	0	0
FHLB line (fully secured)	0	0	0	0	0	0	0	0	0	0	0
Less: outstanding	0	0	0	0	0	0	0	0	0	0	0
Other borrowing lines (fully secured)	0	0	0	0	0	0	0	0	0	0	0
Less: outstanding	0	0	0	0	0	0	0	0	0	0	0
Available securities (market value)	0	0	0	0	0	0	0	0	0	0	0
Other (detail)	0	0	0	0	0	0	0	0	0	0	0
Total	**0**	**0**	**0**	**0**	**0**	**0**	**0**	**0**	**0**	**0**	**0**
Less:											
Reserve requirement	0	0	0	0	0	0	0	0	0	0	0
TT&L	0	0	0	0	0	0	0	0	0	0	0
Minimum balance requirements	0	0	0	0	0	0	0	0	0	0	0
Other (detail)	0	0	0	0	0	0	0	0	0	0	0
Total	**0**	**0**	**0**	**0**	**0**	**0**	**0**	**0**	**0**	**0**	**0**
Total available liquidity	**0**	**0**	**0**	**0**	**0**	**0**	**0**	**0**	**0**	**0**	**0**

Time horizon	Period − 5	Period − 4	Period − 3	Period − 2	Period − 1	Current period	Period + 1	Period + 2	Period + 3	Period + 4	Period + 5
Sensitive funding											
CDs > $250,000	0	0	0	0	0	0	0	0	0	0	0
DDAs > $250,000	0	0	0	0	0	0	0	0	0	0	0
Savings > $250,000	0	0	0	0	0	0	0	0	0	0	0
MMDAs > $250,000	0	0	0	0	0	0	0	0	0	0	0
Other sensitive depositors (detail)	0	0	0	0	0	0	0	0	0	0	0
Brokered deposits (including CDARS)	0	0	0	0	0	0	0	0	0	0	0
Deposits gathered via listing service	0	0	0	0	0	0	0	0	0	0	0
Public funds (secured)	0	0	0	0	0	0	0	0	0	0	0
Public funds (unsecured)	0	0	0	0	0	0	0	0	0	0	0
Other large depositors (> x% of total deposits)	0	0	0	0	0	0	0	0	0	0	0
Other uninsured deposits (> x% of total deposits)	0	0	0	0	0	0	0	0	0	0	0
Other sensitive funds providers (detail)	0	0	0	0	0	0	0	0	0	0	0
Total sensitive funding	**0**	**0**	**0**	**0**	**0**	**0**	**0**	**0**	**0**	**0**	**0**
Available liquidity as a % of deposits	0.00%	0.00%	0.00%	0.00%	0.00%	0.00%	0.00%	0.00%	0.00%	0.00%	0.00%
Available liquidity as a % of sensitive funding	0.00%	0.00%	0.00%	0.00%	0.00%	0.00%	0.00%	0.00%	0.00%	0.00%	0.00%
Available liquidity as a % of total liabilities	0.00%	0.00%	0.00%	0.00%	0.00%	0.00%	0.00%	0.00%	0.00%	0.00%	0.00%

Comments and assumptions:

Appendix H: Example—National Bank
Problem Bank—Cash Flow Trend Report
September 30, 20XX

Reported in (000s)

Time horizon	Period – 5	Period – 4	Period – 3	Period – 2	Period – 1	Current period	Period + 1	Period + 2	Period + 3	Period + 4	Period + 5
Source of funds from operations											
Loan collections (P&I)	0	0	0	0	0	0	0	0	0	0	0
Loan sale activities	0	0	0	0	0	0	0	0	0	0	0
Investment collections (P&I)	0	0	0	0	0	0	0	0	0	0	0
Investment/asset sales :	0	0	0	0	0	0	0	0	0	0	0
Other operating source of funds	0	0	0	0	0	0	0	0	0	0	0
Use of funds from operations											
Loan originations	0	0	0	0	0	0	0	0	0	0	0
Investment/asset purchases	0	0	0	0	0	0	0	0	0	0	0
Operating and interest expense	0	0	0	0	0	0	0	0	0	0	0
Other operating use of funds	0	0	0	0	0	0	0	0	0	0	0
Wire transfer activity (not reported elsewhere)	0	0	0	0	0	0	0	0	0	0	0
Total net cash flow from operations	0	0	0	0	0	0	0	0	0	0	0
Net deposit activity											
Net change in demand deposits	0	0	0	0	0	0	0	0	0	0	0
Net change in brokered deposits	0	0	0	0	0	0	0	0	0	0	0
Brokered deposit maturities	0	0	0	0	0	0	0	0	0	0	0
Net deposit activity	0	0	0	0	0	0	0	0	0	0	0
Net operations and deposit funds	0	0	0	0	0	0	0	0	0	0	0

Reported in (000s)

Time horizon	Period −5	Period −4	Period −3	Period −2	Period −1	Current period	Period +1	Period +2	Period +3	Period +4	Period +5
Borrowing maturities											
Federal funds purchased maturities	0	0	0	0	0	0	0	0	0	0	0
Repurchase agreement maturities	0	0	0	0	0	0	0	0	0	0	0
FHLB borrowing maturities	0	0	0	0	0	0	0	0	0	0	0
FRB discount window maturities	0	0	0	0	0	0	0	0	0	0	0
Other borrowing maturities	0	0	0	0	0	0	0	0	0	0	0
Total borrowing maturities	0	0	0	0	0	0	0	0	0	0	0
Cash needed from financing activities	0	0	0	0	0	0	0	0	0	0	0
Estimated borrowing capacity											
Available balances from federal funds	0	0	0	0	0	0	0	0	0	0	0
Lines of credit	0	0	0	0	0	0	0	0	0	0	0
Brokered CDs	0	0	0	0	0	0	0	0	0	0	0
Available repurchase agreement capacity	0	0	0	0	0	0	0	0	0	0	0
Available FHLB capacity	0	0	0	0	0	0	0	0	0	0	0
Available FRB discount window capacity	0	0	0	0	0	0	0	0	0	0	0
Total estimated borrowing capacity	0	0	0	0	0	0	0	0	0	0	0
Total change in cash	0	0	0	0	0	0	0	0	0	0	0
Beginning cash	0	0	0	0	0	0	0	0	0	0	0
Ending cash	0	0	0	0	0	0	0	0	0	0	0
Other unencumbered, readily marketable assets	0	0	0	0	0	0	0	0	0	0	0

Comments and assumptions:

Appendix I: Joint Agency Advisory on Brokered and Rate-Sensitive Deposits
(Released May 11, 2001, With OCC Advisory Letter AL 2001-5, Since Rescinded)

Office of the Comptroller of the Currency
Board of Governors of the Federal Reserve System
Federal Deposit Insurance Corporation
Office of Thrift Supervision

Joint Agency Advisory on Brokered and Rate-Sensitive Deposits

Purpose

The Office of the Comptroller of the Currency, the Federal Reserve Board, the Federal Deposit Insurance Corporation (FDIC), and the Office of Thrift Supervision (the Agencies) are reminding bankers and examiners of the potential risks associated with excessive reliance on brokered and other highly rate-sensitive deposits, such as those obtained through the Internet, certificate of deposit listing services, and similar advertising programs. When prudently managed, these deposits can be and often are beneficial to banks. However, without proper monitoring and management, they may be an unstable source of funding for an institution. This issuance outlines prudent risk identification and management for rate-sensitive deposits. It applies to all FDIC insured commercial and savings institutions ("banks")[1].

Background

Deposit brokers have traditionally provided intermediary services for banks and investors. Recent developments in technology provide bankers increased access to a broad range of potential investors who have no relationship with the bank and who actively seek the highest returns offered within the financial industry. In particular, the Internet and other automated service providers are effectively and efficiently matching yield-focused investors with potentially high-yielding deposits. Typically, banks offer certificates of deposit (CDs) tailored to the $100,000 FDIC deposit insurance limit to eliminate credit risk to the investor, but amounts may exceed insurance coverage. Rates paid on these deposits are often higher than those paid for local market area retail CDs, but due to the FDIC insurance coverage, these rates may be lower than for unsecured wholesale market funding.

Customers who focus exclusively on rates are highly rate-sensitive and provide less stable funding than do those with local retail deposit relationships. These rate-sensitive customers have easy access to, and are frequently well informed about, alternative markets and investments, and may have no other relationship with or loyalty to the bank. If market conditions change or more attractive returns become available, these customers may rapidly transfer their funds to new institutions or investments. Rate-sensitive customers with deposits in excess of the insurance limits also may be alert to and sensitive to changes in a bank's financial condition. Accordingly, these rate-sensitive depositors, both under and over the $100,000 FDIC insurance limit, may exhibit characteristics more typical of wholesale investors.

---

[1] This guidance supplements each agency's existing supervisory and examination guidance on funding and liquidity issues.

1

Under 12 USC 1831f and 12CFR 337.6, determination of "brokered" status is based initially on whether a bank actually obtains a deposit directly or indirectly through a deposit broker. Banks that are considered only "adequately capitalized" under the "Prompt Corrective Action" (PCA) standard[2] must receive a waiver from the FDIC before they can accept, renew, or roll over any brokered deposit. They also are restricted in the rates they may offer on such deposits. Banks falling below the adequately capitalized range may not accept, renew, or roll over any brokered deposit nor solicit deposits with an effective yield more than 75 basis points above the prevailing market rate. These restrictions will reduce the availability of funding alternatives as a bank's condition deteriorates. Bank managers who use brokered deposits should be familiar with the regulation governing brokered deposits and understand the requirements for requesting a waiver.

Deposits attracted over the Internet, through CD listing services, or through special advertising programs offering premium rates to customers without another banking relationship, also require special monitoring. Although these deposits may not fall within the technical definition of "brokered" in 12 USC 1831f and 12 CFR 337.6, their inherent risk characteristics are similar to brokered deposits[3]. That is, such deposits are typically attractive to rate-sensitive customers who may not have significant loyalty to the bank. Extensive reliance on funding products of this type, especially those obtained from outside a bank's geographic market area, has the potential to weaken a bank's funding position.

Some banks have used brokered and Internet-based funding to support rapid growth in loans and other assets. Bankers are reminded that under the Agencies' safety and soundness standards[4], a bank's asset growth should be prudent and its management must consider the source, volatility, and use of the funds generated to support asset growth.

Risk Management Guidelines

The Agencies expect bank management to implement risk management systems commensurate in complexity with the liquidity and funding risks undertaken. Such systems should incorporate the following principles:

- **Proper funds management policies.** A good policy should generally provide for forward planning, establish an appropriate cost structure, and set realistic limitations and business strategies. It should clearly convey the board's risk tolerance and should not be ambiguous about who holds responsibility for funds management decisions.

---

[2] See 12 CFR Part 325, Subpart B for FDIC insured institutions, 12 CFR 6.4 for national banks, 12 CFR 208.40 for state member banks, or 12 CFR Part 565 for thrift institutions.
[3] Moreover, under 12 CFR 337.6(a)(5)(iii), the restrictions on brokered deposits do apply to solicitations by a depository institution that is less than well-capitalized where the solicitation offers rates of interest "significantly higher" than the prevailing rates of interest in the institution's "normal market area." This can be particularly problematic for Internet solicitations since determination of the bank's "normal market area" for such deposits is difficult.
[4] See 12 CFR 364 for FDIC insured institutions, 12 CFR 30 Appendix A for national banks, 12 CFR 208 Appendix D-1 for state member banks, or 12 CFR Part 570 for thrift institutions.

2

- **Adequate due diligence when assessing deposit brokers.** Bank management should implement adequate due diligence procedures before entering any business relationship with a deposit broker. Deposit brokers are not regulated by the Agencies.

- **Due diligence in assessing the potential risk to earnings and capital associated with brokered or other rate-sensitive deposits, and prudent strategies for their use.** Bankers should manage highly sensitive funding sources carefully, avoiding excessive reliance on funds that may be only temporarily available or which may require premium rates to retain.

- **Reasonable control structures to limit funding concentrations.** Limit structures should consider typical behavioral patterns for depositors or investors and be designed to control excessive reliance on any significant source(s) or type of funding. This includes brokered funds, and other rate-sensitive or credit-sensitive deposits obtained through Internet or other types of advertising.

- **Management information systems (MIS) that clearly identify non-relationship or higher-cost funding programs and allow management to track performance, manage funding gaps, and monitor compliance with concentration and other risk limits.** At a minimum, MIS should include a listing of funds obtained through each significant program, rates paid on each instrument and an average per program, information on maturity of the instruments, and concentration or other limit monitoring and reporting. Management should also ensure that brokered deposits are properly reported in Consolidated Reports of Condition and Income[5].

- **Contingency funding plans that address the risk that these deposits may not "roll over" and provide a reasonable alternative funding strategy.** Contingency funding plans should factor in the potential for changes in market acceptance if reduced rates are offered on rate-sensitive deposits. The potential for triggering legal limitations that restrict the bank's access to brokered deposits under Prompt Corrective Action standards, and the effect that this would have on the bank's liability structure, should also be factored into the plan.

Examination Guidelines

Examiners should carefully assess the liquidity risk management framework at all banks. Banks with meaningful reliance on brokered or other rate-sensitive deposits should receive the appropriate level of supervisory attention. Examiners should not wait for PCA provisions to be triggered, or the viability of the institution to be in question, before raising relevant safety and soundness issues with regard to the use of these funding sources. If a determination is made that a bank's use of these funding sources is not safe and sound, or that these risks are excessive or that they adversely affect the condition of the institution, then appropriate supervisory action should be immediately taken. The following represent potential red flags that may indicate the need to take action to ensure the risks associated with brokered or other rate-sensitive funding sources are managed appropriately:

---

[5] See Instructions for Consolidated Reports of Condition and Income, schedule RC-E - Deposits.

3

- Ineffective management or the absence of appropriate expertise,
- Newly chartered institution with few relationship deposits and an aggressive growth strategy,
- Inadequate internal audit coverage,
- Inadequate information systems or controls,
- Identified or suspected fraud,
- High on- or off-balance-sheet growth rates,
- Use of rate-sensitive funds not in keeping with the bank's strategy,
- Inadequate consideration of risk, with management focus exclusively on rates,
- Significant funding shifts from traditional funding sources,
- The absence of adequate policy limitations on these kinds of funding sources,
- High loan delinquency rate or deterioration in other asset quality indicators,
- Deterioration in the general financial condition of the institution, and
- Other conditions or circumstances warranting the need for administrative action.

4

Liquidity References

Laws

12 USC 56, Prohibition on Withdrawal of Capital; Unearned Dividends
12 USC 60, Dividends
12 USC 90, Depositories of Public Moneys and Financial Agents of Government
12 USC 371c (d)(1), Restrictions on Transactions With Affiliates
12 USC 501 and 18 USC 1004, Certification of Checks
12 USC 1821, Insurance Funds
12 USC 1831f, Brokered Deposits
12 USC 1831f-1, Deposit Broker Notification and Record Keeping
12 USC 1831o, Prompt Corrective Action
15 USC 77c (a) (3), Commercial Paper Definition Escheat Laws (Local)
Uniform Commercial Code (UCC) 4-107, 211, 212, 301, and 302, Banking Hours and Processing of Demand Items

Regulations

12 CFR 5, Rules, Policies, and Procedures for Corporate Activities
12 CFR 6, Prompt Corrective Action
12 CFR 7.4002 (a), Charges by Banks
12 CFR 7.4002 (b), Service Charges on Dormant Accounts
12 CFR 21.11, Known or Suspected Theft, Embezzlement, Check-Kiting Operation, Defalcation
12 CFR 31 Deposits Between Affiliated Banks (Appendix A, Section 2)
12 CFR 32.3(c)(1), Loans Not Subject to Lending Limit
12 CFR 201, Extensions of Credit by Federal Reserve Banks (Regulation A)
12 CFR 204, Regulation D, Reserve Requirements of Depository Institutions
12 CFR 206, Regulation F, Limitations on Interbank Liabilities
12 CFR 337.6, Brokered Deposits
12 CFR 935, Federal Housing Finance Board, Advances
31 CFR 203.9 and 203.10, Treasury Tax and Loan
31 CFR 210, Federal Recurring Payments Through Financial Institutions

Issuances

Comptroller's Handbook, "Asset Securitization"
Comptroller's Handbook, "Community Bank Supervision"

Comptroller's Handbook, "Federal Branches and Agencies"
Comptroller's Handbook, "Interest Rate Risk"
Comptroller's Handbook, "Investment Securities"
Comptroller's Handbook, "Large Bank Supervision"
Comptroller's Handbook, "Risk Management of Financial Derivatives"
Consolidated Reports of Condition and Income (call reports) in Debt and Equity Securities
"Joint Agency Advisory on Brokered and Rate-Sensitive Deposits"
OCC 2002-22, "Capital Treatment of Recourse, Direct Credit Substitutes, and Residual Interests in Asset Securitization"
OCC 2003-36, "Interagency Advisory on the Use of Federal Reserve's Primary Credit Program in Effective Liquidity Management"
OCC 2004-02, "Banks/Thrifts Providing Financial Support to Funds Advised by the Banking Organization or its Affiliates: Interagency Guidance"
OCC 2005-26, "Regulatory Capital: Asset-Based Commercial Paper Liquidity Facilities: Interagency Guidance"
OCC 2007-21, "Supervision of National Trust Banks: Revised Guidance: Capital and Liquidity"
OCC 2010-13, "Interagency Policy Statement on Funding and Liquidity Risk Management"
OCC 2010-16, "Correspondent Concentration Risks"
OCC 2011-12, "Supervisory Guidance on Model Risk Management"

Other Guidance

Basel Committee on Banking Supervision, "Principles for Sound Liquidity Risk Management and Supervision," September 2008
Basel Committee on Banking Supervision, "Basel III: International Framework for Liquidity Risk Measurement, Standards, and Monitoring," December 2010

www.ingramcontent.com/pod-product-compliance
Lightning Source LLC
Chambersburg PA
CBHW080519290526
45790CB00006B/2231